THE COBBLER

THE COBBLER

HOW I DISRUPTED AN INDUSTRY, FELL FROM GRACE, AND CAME BACK STRONGER THAN EVER

STEVE MADDEN

with JODI LIPPER

RADIUS BOOK GROUP
NEW YORK

Distributed by Radius Book Group
A Division of Diversion Publishing Corp.
443 Park Avenue South, Suite 1004
New York, NY 10016
www.RadiusBookGroup.com

This memoir is a truthful recollection of the formative events in the author's life. The events, places, and conversations in this memoir have been re-created from memory. The dialogue does not represent a word-for-word transcript of what was discussed, but in all instances the essence of conversations is accurate. In order to maintain the anonymity of certain people involved, some names and identifying details have been changed.

For more information, email info@radiusbookgroup.com.

First edition: May 2020
Hardcover ISBN: 978-1-63576-695-0
eBook ISBN: 978-1-63576-691-2

Manufactured in the United States of America

10 9 8 7 6 5 4 3 2

Cover design by Matthew Ellenberger
Interior design by Neuwirth & Associates, Inc.

Radius Book Group and the Radius Book Group colophon are registered trademarks of Radius Book Group, a Division of Diversion Publishing Corp.

For my brother Luke, who inspired and
influenced me in so many ways.
I love you.

"If you're going through hell, keep going."

—ATTRIBUTED TO WINSTON CHURCHILL

CONTENTS

THE COBBLER

INTRODUCTION

I fidgeted in my tux, restless as ever, as the supermodel Winnie Harlow stood onstage talking about my career, my brand, and me. These events always felt surreal. I never got used to them, and it was hard to focus on what she was saying as thoughts flooded through my brain. *Is my jacket straight? Do I have all the notes for my speech? It's nice that Winnie is wearing a pair of my shoes.*

"Steve Madden has been called many things," Winnie said from the podium. *That's for sure*, I thought.

"Mogul," she said, pausing for effect. "Icon."

I could have added to that list. As a kid, I was called things like stupid and lazy, a pain in the ass who couldn't shut up and sit still. Nobody knew then that I had an attention disorder that kept me from focusing, or that such a thing even existed. In my teens and twenties, I was called other things: a partier, a wild man. But at the height of my addiction, when I was either out crashing cars or hiding in my apartment, isolating myself from the world, my life was anything but a party.

It wasn't until I turned thirty and got clean that people started calling me things that were positive: creative, charismatic, someone who was on the pulse of trends and knew how to create a cool product for a good price. When I look back, those years were the best—hustling and fighting, clawing my way to the top of an industry that was loathe to accept an outsider like me. But they were also the years when I made my biggest mistakes fueled by impatience and a replacement addiction: money. After my downfall, the names I was called were the most hurtful, even though they were true: a criminal, a convict, a mere number as far as anyone running the facility I was locked up in cared to know.

And now, years later, here I was in a fancy ballroom wearing a tuxedo and receiving an award for creating a multi-billion-dollar global brand. Looking back at both the past thirty years and that last sentence, it seems like nothing more than an illusion, a random twist of fate that landed me here. But can life possibly be that cruel?

"And tonight," Winnie said with a big smile, turning to the spot where I stood offstage, "we add visionary to that list." I walked onto the stage, and she presented me with a small figurine of a clutch covered in Swarovski crystals—the Accessories Council's Visionary Award.

The rest of the night was a blur of mingling and congratulations. A few hours later, it was a relief to be home on the Upper East Side of Manhattan.

On a clear day, I can see from my apartment over the bridge to Queens, New York, where I was born. My family soon moved a stone's throw away to the Five Towns of Long Island, a place that is still very much a part of me, from my accent to my style (or lack thereof) to my lingering sense of being just slightly left of center.

The Five Towns is where I found my two great loves: shoes and golf. I'm not a very good athlete, but I have always loved sports. In high school, I didn't make the school's basketball team, so I played on an intramural team just for fun. I was probably the worst player on the team, but I enjoyed it, and it gave me an outlet for my restless energy.

When I was growing up, the Five Towns was a prototypical Jewish suburb. But one of those five towns, Inwood, was home to mostly black, Italian, and Irish Catholic families. The neighborhoods were essentially segregated, as much of the country was back then, but our high school was mixed. Before basketball season started, I heard that a group of black guys had been kicked off of the varsity team for smoking weed or some other bullshit reason. I'd been friends with those guys since we were kids. They were unbelievably talented athletes who worked hard. Watching them play basketball was like seeing Mikhail Baryshnikov dance. Beautiful. It was a no-brainer to ask them to join the intramural team.

With the help of our new teammates, we dominated throughout the season and went from one of the worst teams in the league to facing off in the championship game. It was obvious that, for us to win, those guys needed as much play time as possible. So, I benched myself and watched with excitement, cheering them on as they masterfully won the game.

When it was time to announce the MVP, I wondered which of our star players would be named. They were all so good, it would be hard to choose. Instead, they called my name. My first thought was that it had to be a mistake. How could I be the most valuable player when I hadn't even played in the game?

As I accepted the trophy in a state of shock, I realized that they were giving me credit for seeing the potential in others and giving their talents a platform. I was the most valuable member because I had put the team together and then stayed out of the way, allowing them to shine.

Fast-forward almost forty-five years later, and I realized that I had won this Visionary Award for doing the exact same thing. For thirty years, in between designing and selling shoes and disrupting the fashion industry, I've been building a team at Steve Madden that is the best in the business. Yes, I've taught and coached them, but I've also been incredibly lucky to surround myself with hardworking, talented people. I never hired based on a specific skill set or kind of experience. My approach is more that of a coach—in particular, Gil Brandt of the Dallas Cowboys, who was famous for making unconventional draft choices based on a player's potential. When I find someone I trust, someone I know will be a good partner, I find a role to fit the person instead of trying to force someone into a specific position.

Then the trick is to let go. The entrepreneur is a control freak and a perfectionist, and the truth is I probably wouldn't have let go if my hand hadn't been forced right at the height of my career when I was sentenced to forty-one months in prison. At that point, I had no choice but to shore up my team, put my faith in them, and step aside. The results speak for themselves. And the irony is that I'm still winning championships by keeping myself out of the game.

It's been a long road from that intramural championship to the Visionary Award. Now, people speak about my accomplishments in the past tense: "How did you do it?"

I know what they're asking. How did I build this brand from nothing and go from childhood screw-up to convict to someone who's being showered with awards? The answer is deceptively simple: I put things together—whether they're shoes, teams, or the disjointed pieces of my life.

Jordan Belfort, the infamous "Wolf of Wall Street," first called me The Cobbler back when we were friends, as he took my company public and invited me to work with him on other deals too. And while that relationship represents one of the biggest mistakes of my life, one that led to a painful downfall, I have to admit that the name he gave me fits in more ways than Jordan ever could have known.

Jordan called me The Cobbler simply because I was obsessed with shoes. But to me it means so much more than that. A cobbler puts the various pieces of a shoe together: the upper, the lower, the lining, and so on. But a real shoe guy knows that shoes are made of more than just raw materials. The inspiration behind the style is just as important and includes references pulled from music, pop culture, and whatever else is going on in the zeitgeist. The result is a shoe that's not just comfortable and well made, but that says something about the person who is wearing it.

I got a thrill out of pulling these various pieces together to create my most iconic styles, from the Marilyn to the Mary Lou, the Slinky, and, more recently, the Troopa. But I've used the same techniques to piece together a team of mostly outsiders, hires that make no sense individually but that are amazingly effective together. And though it's hard to separate the company from my life, that's been pieced together, too, and thanks to my kids and friends and the people I love, it's now mostly whole.

So, which one am I: the egomaniac, the trend spotter, the entrepreneur, or the visionary? What about the family man? Honestly, they're all true. I'm the same flawed person I've always been. In fact, the more successful I've become, the less sure of anything I have grown. When I was young and just starting out, I thought I had all the answers. Hard work and money were all that mattered. Success at all costs would be worth it. Now, I'm not so sure. I have money. I have success. And I've paid for it by losing years of my life and people I loved. Was it worth it?

My answer is an unequivocal *yes*. It may sound like an overstatement, but if I could go back, I wouldn't change a moment, even the time I spent in prison, thinking my life was over. Whether it's a shoe or a life, without each piece carefully stitched together, the final product will never be the same.

But I want you to read my story and tell me what you think. What would you have done differently? My success may or may not be an illusion, but the hustle, the hard work, and the costs it took for me to get here could not have been more real. It was a wild ride. Maybe you'll learn something. If not, I'm pretty sure you'll be entertained. All I can promise is to hold nothing back as I cobble the pieces of my story together.

01
SEAT

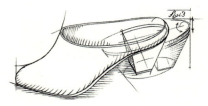

seat • where the heel of the foot sits in the shoe.
it normally matches the shape of the heel for comfort and support.

Growing up, I always felt like an outsider. The kids I went to school with were almost all from the same type of upper-middle-class Jewish families, but I was different. My dad was Irish Catholic and from the "other side of the tracks," while my mother was a local Jewish girl. I was the only mixed, half-Jewish kid to be found.

This isn't rare today. My kids go to school, and everyone's half-Jewish. But it was incredibly rare back then. The folks from my father's neighborhood of Inwood, with its small lots and squat, modest houses, were the cabbies and bartenders who served the wealthier residents of the other neighborhoods. Those towns were filled with grander homes on wider, tree-lined streets. Our house was relatively modest with a nice-sized yard on the side where my brothers and I played football and a smaller yard in the back where my mother kept a tomato garden.

There wasn't a lot of tension between the folks in Inwood and the rest of the Five Towns, but there wasn't much mixing, either. I grew up in the 1960s and '70s, the height of the civil rights era, and crossing that line was still considered risqué. Jewish kids didn't hang out with the kids from Inwood. Dating or marrying across the line was basically unheard of. Except for my parents.

This meant there was nobody else in my neighborhood like me. I was a complete anomaly, but it didn't bother me. In fact, I reveled in it. I didn't have to pay much of a price for my differences. They weren't big enough for me to be ostracized, just for a friend's mom to look at me sideways every once in a while. For the most part, I was free to enjoy my outsider status. It gave me the freedom to be whoever I wanted.

There was no mold for me to try to fit into. It would have been impossible for me to be like the Jewish kids I hung out with or like the kids from Inwood. So, I pulled from the people around me and cobbled together those disparate elements to become my own person.

As a kid, I idolized my dad. Now, long after he's passed, I'm more fascinated by him. Much of his family worked in the Catholic Church, and he left all that behind to assimilate into a Jewish family and lifestyle. He even partnered up with other Jewish guys to run a little textile company, Abbott Fabrics. And he was the most Irish Catholic–looking dude around, tall and distinguished with a full head of silver hair. He looked like a Supreme Court justice, not a *schnorrer* working in the Garment District. But nonetheless, there he was.

My dad was already forty-four and my mom was thirty-six when I was born, the youngest of three boys. My parents had grown up during the Depression and were in their twenties during World War II. They knew what it was like to lose everything, including family members who went off to war and never came back. My friends' parents were only kids during World War II. They were born into a period of great hope and optimism, rather than one of the darkest times in our country. I could feel this difference when I visited my friends' homes. The air felt lighter, breezier. Hugs and compliments were given out more freely, and money flowed more liberally too.

Being exposed to such a wide range of generations affected me in ways I wouldn't fully understand until I was much older. When it came to my business, I've always had an old-school, blue-collar mentality.

From day one, my team and I were scrappy and worked on a shoestring, pulling ourselves up by our bootstraps, if you will. This I learned from my father. But I paired that old-fashioned work ethic with a hip, forward-thinking approach to the design and marketing of my shoes. This aspect of the business was influenced by both my older brothers' generation and my own, and later by the young men and women I hired to help marry the past with the future.

My father worked hard, but the textile business was tough. He never made the big bucks, and the overall feeling in my house when I was a kid was that we might lose everything at any moment. Every weekend, my father would sit me down and read me the bankruptcy notices in the newspaper. "Look at what is happening in this country!" he would tell me.

Looking back, I don't think we were really that close to going broke. We certainly weren't rich, but we weren't poor, either. I had a bike, but never a Schwinn like most of my friends in town. The Five Towns was an economically competitive place, and we struggled to keep up with our neighbors. My dad worked hard, though, and earned enough to buy a Cadillac and to play golf on the weekends. Golf was his respite, and I inferred that he had to play golf on the weekends to have the energy to work so hard during the week.

Even with these small comforts, my parents had been so traumatized by what they'd seen during the Depression that they lived in constant fear of poverty. There was a lot of fear in our house: fear of the floor falling out from beneath us and fear of my father's temper. He was the center of our world, and his mood dictated exactly what went on in my family. If he was in a good mood, things were great. He'd take me to a football game and sing the national anthem at the top of his lungs. It embarrassed the hell out of me, but a part of me secretly loved it. If he was in a bad mood, though, look out.

My dad was something of an egomaniac—he drank too much, and he was hard on me, but he was a good man. I may have judged my father harshly when I was younger, but now I see him for what he was: a poor boy who never went to college, who was cut off from his family, and who worked like a dog to provide for his kids. He taught me my single most valuable business lesson, and that is, *first things first*. You have to take care of the fundamentals—putting food on the table, paying your bills—before anything else. He lived by that rule, and from the moment I started my business, I have too.

I realize I haven't said much about my mother, and that's because my childhood was my father's show, not hers. As a little boy, the time I spent with her still revolved around my dad. Every evening, we'd drive to the train station to pick him up after a long day of work. There was no need for him to call my mom to tell her when to leave the house. He took the same train every night. I remember sitting in the back seat of our Cadillac eagerly waiting to see him walk off of the train in his long coat and hat.

Looking back, I can see that my mother had a creative side of her own. We had a piano in the house, and she would hear a song on the radio, jump on the piano, and pick out the notes herself, playing it by ear. It was incredible. But between my father's moods and managing three boys, she didn't have much chance to pursue her own interests. This was, unfortunately, the case for many women of her generation. Unlike my friends' moms, though, mine wasn't at all a typical, overbearing, Jewish mother. In fact, she showed little interest in me.

I don't know if this was because I was the third kid or because she didn't particularly care for me. I recognize now that she loved me, but it was clear to me from a young age that my mom didn't really *like* me. And I can't entirely blame her. I was a hyper, skinny little loud-mouthed kid who was always getting into trouble, and my mom had no patience for it. My grandmother on my mother's side, who lived with us for a while, would say in Yiddish that I had *shpilkes*, a nervous energy or an inability to sit still. Everyone else just said I was a pain in the ass.

At school, I got in trouble for constantly speaking out of turn, for tapping my hands on the desk, and for being a class clown. I was impulsive, and I couldn't stop my mouth from interrupting the teacher or making a wisecrack even if I'd tried. At home, I was just as loud and obnoxious, a smart-ass.

My mom couldn't stand me, but my dad tolerated me a bit more. Maybe this was because I tried to tone it down around him, ever wary of his mood. I only succeeded sometimes. Nobody imagined that I had some sort of attention deficit or learning disorder. There was no such thing back then, really. You were either a good kid or a bad one, and I was definitely the latter.

As I absorbed the disappointment of my mother and my teachers, I made a caricature out of myself. It wasn't a conscious decision, but I had been written the role of troublemaker, and I played right into it. I broke the rules and acted obnoxiously just to prove them right. There was a moment that this flipped, but that came much later, around the time I started the business. At that point, the same urge to act out mutated into an intense work ethic and obsessive drive to succeed at all costs in order to prove them wrong. Unfortunately, it took decades of screwing up before I could make this shift.

As a kid, there were two times I could focus: when I was reading and when I was playing golf. I never did well in school, but I was an avid reader, and I especially loved biographies of movie moguls like Louis B. Mayer and Samuel Goldwyn. There was something about the intersection of art and commerce that intrigued me even then. These guys were interested in the whole vision of a project from beginning to end. They were businessmen like my father who went to the office in a suit and tie every day, but they were also artists. That was a completely new concept to me.

I was fascinated to read about the guy who made *Gone with the Wind*. He wasn't the director. He didn't write the screenplay. He wasn't an actor.

His name was David O. Selznick, and he was the executive producer. That's who I wanted to be: the person who put all the pieces of a project together. But in my house, there was no value placed on being creative. If someone went to an easel and painted, then they were creative. But who cared? Hard work was what mattered, not creativity.

Now I know that creativity encompasses so much more than just making art. It's an ability to lead, to hustle, to see around corners and predict future trends and problems, and, yes, to create, as well. As a kid, it wouldn't even have occurred to me to think of myself as creative, and I still have days when I wonder if I really am. At the same time, I can see now that my artistic spirit made me sensitive to the environment around me and able to take in so much stimuli.

Besides my dad, I absorbed the most from my two older brothers. John was eleven years older than me, and Luke was three years younger than John. This meant that by the time I was seven years old, I was practically an only child. John left for college, and Luke was cutting class and flunking out of high school, so my parents sent him off to boarding school.

My dad was in his fifties by then, and he and my mom seemed ready to be finished with the hard work of parenting. They'd already been doing it for so long. I was left to my own devices much of the time. On the weekends I rode my bike all over town with my friends, and over the summer they sent me to sleep-away camp.

It was at camp that I started to use my full field of vision and natural awareness of the people around me. I could see clearly who could use a pick-me-up and who was feeling invisible and needed me to throw a little attention their way. The summer I was ten, we took popularity votes every night in our bunk. Don't ask me why. In the morning I'd choose someone who seemed like he needed a boost and spend the day trying to help him get voted the most popular.

"Can you believe how Bobby landed that volleyball serve?" I'd ask the group of kids as we roasted hot dogs over a bonfire. "He really helped us win that one." Of course, building up the people around me was also my way of making sure I was liked myself. This was something that mattered to me more than I would have admitted or even been able to understand.

During the school year, I played baseball or basketball with my friends every day after school. I spent much of that time doing the same things I did at camp: emphasizing other people's talents and making the rest of the team feel good. On the weekends, I golfed with my dad. That was our thing, and thanks to my dad, golf became a huge part of my life. It was also the one sport I really excelled at.

I wish I could remember what my dad and I talked about while we golfed. Probably not much, really. But I do remember how strict he was about making sure I raked the bunker after we took our shots. Overall, he wasn't a strict father. He drilled his work ethic into me and then left me to figure out the rest for myself. But if I ever forgot to rake the bunker, forget it. He'd totally lose it on me, and our golf game would be ruined. Now, every time I rake the bunker, I feel like I'm having a little moment with my dad.

Once in a while, my dad would take me to work with him in Manhattan. We'd board the train in Long Island, and when we got out at Penn Station—*boom!* We were in another world. I loved it. There were businessmen in suits like my dad, running to catch their trains, shoeshine guys calling out to us, and a newsstand run by an old blind man. I remember giving him change for the newspaper. He could tell right away how much money I had given him just by the feel of the coins. I watched in awe one day as he cursed out a guy who had given him a penny instead of a quarter, trying to stiff him on the paper.

Then we'd exit the train station on Thirty-Fourth Street and walk up to the Garment District. It was a rush. There were people and noise and colors everywhere, a perfect replica of the chaos in my mind. At age ten, I vowed to live in the city one day.

I hardly remember a time when I lived in the same house as my brothers, but that doesn't mean that they had any less of an influence on me. I got a dual education from my parents on one side and my brothers on the other. John and Luke were very different from each other. At least, this seemed to be the case back then. John was simply the coolest guy ever, and I idolized him just as much, if not more, than my dad. He was unbelievably charismatic and handsome, impeccably dressed, and had an innate ability to charm everyone he met. The guys all loved him, the girls went nuts for him, and he was a nice guy on top of it too. I worshipped him, and I wasn't alone. Everyone in the Five Towns thought Johnny Madden was a god, and it was a boon for me to be able to walk into a room and have everyone know I was his little brother.

While John was charming and sophisticated, Luke was fully immersed in the hippie counterculture. And I don't mean that he just wore bellbottoms and smelled like patchouli. There were people who were influenced by hippies, and then there were the hippies themselves. Luke was the real deal. When I was eleven or twelve, he left college and moved to a commune in Baltimore. The next time we saw him, he was unrecognizable. Not just the way he looked, but the way he acted and talked, his whole demeanor. It was all peace, love, drugs, and long hair. It wasn't my thing, but I thought it was cool. My parents, though, just looked at him like he was an alien, a freak.

I loved both my brothers, despite, or perhaps because of, their differences. From John, I took the value of charm and likeability, but I soaked in Luke's whole vibe too. The music, the fashion, the free spirit, and the focus on love and acceptance were all beautiful to me. I was younger and more a part of the Alex P. Keaton generation, but I was shaped by all of it. My trademark penny loafers and long, flowing strawberry blond hair became symbols of my dual influences: my two older brothers.

As the years passed, though, it turned out that John, Luke, and I had more in common than any of us would have expected. Each of us has faced our own slightly different battle as part of the same larger war with alcoholism and addiction. It's a tough fight, one you can never really win outright. The sad truth is that to some extent both my brothers lost their battles. I'm still fighting mine a day at a time.

If you had seen John at the age of twenty or even thirty, you never would have imagined that he'd end up the way he did. He was like an idealized image of a man come to life, and I often asked myself why I couldn't be more like him. But his addiction ate away at him slowly, not fully taking hold until he hit middle age. It kills me that his kids never really had a chance to know him when he was younger. He was the best father he could be, and I know how much his kids loved him, but he was a completely different person by the time they were old enough to remember.

Luke's path may have been easier to predict in some ways because of the hippie thing, but, like John, his alcoholism didn't take over his life until much later, long after the commune and Woodstock were in the history books. Then, despite our family's efforts to help, he fell prey to his disease too.

I'm not judging either of my brothers. I still battle this demon every single day. In a way, it's a blessing that I fell into the clutches of drugs instead of alcohol because they took me out much quicker than booze alone might have. I was a full decade younger than either John or Luke when I hit bottom and knew that I had to get clean or forfeit the entire war.

Where did it come from, this tendency or genetic disease or whatever you want to call it? I often revisit my memories looking for answers. Growing up, alcohol was ever-present in our home. It was never really a problem, but it can't be a coincidence that my father's three sons all turned out to be addicts. He definitely liked to drink, probably too much. Like many men of his generation, he enjoyed his martini lunches. But he always functioned, worked hard, and never made a public scene. No matter what, he was on that same train every night.

In all the times I spent with my dad on the golf course, I don't remember seeing a bottle. But when I was thirteen, I was able to get a junior membership to the golf club, which meant I started playing less with my dad and more with my buddies. Did things get worse after that? Was my father hiding an addiction that fueled his temper and dictated his mood swings and his severe views on life? I'll never know.

The next year, when I was fourteen, I started working as a caddy at the golf course. For five hours a day, I carried two huge bags that each felt like they were bigger than me, and for that I earned fourteen dollars. It was dreadful. Sometimes I caddied for my dad, but I always wished that I was playing with him, instead. The one thing I liked about the job was the opportunity to be around other men my dad's age. I always loved listening to them talk about business and politics and the news of the day.

I found myself uniquely situated to take in the message from the older generation to work hard and the opposite ideology from the younger generation to opt out. I've done both, and this duality has shaped my life and my business. In high school it seemed like I was heading more in the direction of opting out. I started cutting class and smoking pot with my crew of buddies pretty much every day. We were like the rat pack: Alan, Dean,* Brian, Barry, Danny, and me. We skipped school to play golf and smoke pot, often at the same time.

In high school, Brian Frank nicknamed me "fog man" because I was always thinking about a thousand things at once. I was also stoned most of the time. I remember walking down the hallway of our school. It was loud and bustling with other kids heading every which way. Brian was talking to me about something, and I could barely hear him because I was too busy juggling so many other thoughts. To me, it felt like it was out of nowhere when he screamed, "Yo, fog man!" and finally got my attention. For a moment, anyway.

---

* This name has been changed.

I was awkward and scattered, and the fake confidence I used to hide my insecurities often came off as cockiness, which turned off a lot of people. At least I had enough confidence to jump when I saw an opportunity. When I was sixteen, I overheard my friend Jeff Melcer talking about how he was up for a job at a shoe store called Toulouse in downtown Cedarhurst near all the shops and restaurants. It sounded a lot better than busting my ass caddying for fourteen dollars a day. Plus, I knew that store. The owner, Lance Rubin, had gone to school with my brother John. This was one of those times when being his little brother really helped me out. I knew that if I went in there and told Lance who I was, he'd probably give me the job over Jeff. And he did.

Lance was cool. He was only twenty-seven, and he owned the store and dabbled in designing shoes too. This was a guy, like the movie moguls I'd always loved reading about, who combined artistry with commerce in an interesting way. He made no bones about being creative. Lance was also a painter and was really an artist at heart, but he was also a businessman. And in this case, a businessman who looked nothing like those movie moguls or like our fathers.

It was 1975, and the fashion industry had just barely started paying attention to young people. Members of the hippie generation were now in their twenties and had their own unique sense of style. Boutiques like Toulouse, with posters on the walls and rock-and-roll music blasting in the store, were springing up all over the country to commercialize that movement and cater to young people. It was revolutionary. Before that, fashion all skewed older. Young people had no other choice than to basically dress like their parents. Toulouse and other stores like it gave them another option.

The first time I walked into Toulouse, I was completely blown away. It was one thing to see Luke decked out in his hippie regalia. He was only one person. This was an entire store filled with the funkiest, most theatrical shoes I had ever seen. On one table sat the original Goody Two

Shoes with their colorful leather and high wooden heels. Some shoes had wilder patterns and platforms instead of heels. Others took things a step further. Inspired by British glam rock, they paired shiny metallics from the 1960s with huge buckles and platforms. Then there were styles that seemed to contradict themselves: patent leather oxford lace-ups with ridiculously high heels, and platforms with contrast stitching to show off the shoe's construction.

And those were just the women's shoes! The men's were just as wild, with three-inch platforms, sequins, and shiny patent leather for them too. I had always worn penny loafers and had never given much thought to shoes. Now I saw that you could choose to express yourself however you wanted through the shoes you wore. And Toulouse offered customers a wide range of expressions.

When I started working at Toulouse, I did not fit in at all. I looked like Richie Cunningham from *Happy Days*: preppy and straitlaced. The only difference was that I already had long hair. At first, I worked in the basement as a stock boy. I was supposed to be sweeping and straightening up, but most of the time I was down there trying on the platform shoes and falling over as I tried to walk.

Gradually, I acclimated to my surroundings. Taking notes from the people I worked with, my jeans went from tapered to bellbottomed, my shirts gained some metallic threads, and the platforms on my shoes got taller. I even learned to walk in them.

It didn't take long for me to make my way up to the sales floor. I didn't ask for permission. One of my strongest beliefs, especially when it comes to business, is that it's better to beg for forgiveness than to ask for permission. And once I was on the floor, I was a good seller, so there was no need for me to apologize or for them to send me back downstairs.

At Toulouse, I started to learn the rhythm of retail: how a woman tries on a shoe, what she's telling you she wants when she twists this way and that in the mirror, whether her mind is made up when she asks to see a certain shoe or you should bring her another color too. It was sort of like dancing or kissing, an intuitive give-and-take. And unlike either of those activities (at least back then), I was good at it.

When a woman came into the store, I'd help her pick out the shoes she was going to wear every day. Those new shoes would change how she walked, how she dressed, and even how she made her way in the world. I got a rush out of helping design her lifestyle in this way.

One day a young girl named Sloan Berman came into the store with her mother. Sloan was thirteen years old and desperately wanted to buy a pair of platform shoes, but her mother refused. "You're too young," she said as she paid for a pair of her own platforms. Sloan slid all the way down to the floor right in front of the checkout area and burst into tears. Her passion for shoes really stuck with me, and thirty years later, I hired Sloan to work for me. She is now the president of our entire handbag division.

Our customers, like Sloan, rubbed off on me, and little by little I became obsessed with shoes too. I began to see what made certain shoes work, why they became hits while others didn't. And I realized that this ability to see the future was a type of creativity in its own right.

This was a game changer for me. It was the first time I thought it might be cool to create something that hadn't been there before, and, just as important, that I might actually be able to. Until then, I had been looking at myself through the eyes of others and concluded that there was something wrong with me. My experience at Toulouse offered me some redemption, a bit of hope that I wouldn't always be good-for-nothing.

But after working at Toulouse for just a couple years, I had to leave it behind to go to college. I had graduated from high school by the skin of my teeth, but where I'm from, college wasn't optional. Everyone went. Even Luke had gone to college before dropping out and heading off to the commune. I picked the University of Miami for no real reason. My brother John had gotten married and moved to Miami the year before, and a few of my buddies from high school were heading there, so it seemed as good a place as any.

Let's be clear. I'm not proud of my behavior over the next several years. In fact, I'm deeply remorseful. I wish I'd had my shit together enough to make the most of my opportunities and really learn something at college; that I had been smart enough to try to live up to my potential. But I believe the truth is never boring, and, sadly, that is pretty much the exact opposite of what was about to happen.

02
OUTSOLE

outsole • the layer of sole that is exposed to the ground. due to the amount of wear and stress this part of the shoe receives, it is usually made of a very durable material. it is also important that it provide enough friction with the floor to prevent the wearer from slipping.

've never been officially diagnosed with ADHD, but as far as I'm concerned, it's an open-and-shut case. As a kid and even as a teenager, I was able to cope with the distractions. My responsibilities were few, and though my restlessness and impulsive behavior landed me in plenty of trouble in school, I knew how to get by.

College was a completely different beast. The very idea of going to multiple classes in different locations in one day, having a completely separate schedule the next day, and then doing various homework and reading assignments for each of those classes . . . forget it. Just forget it. There was a zero percent chance of me succeeding in that environment. None at all.

It was as if there were four television screens in my mind, each playing a different film. Focusing on one at a time was never an option, but to some extent, I could take in all four of them at once. On an intuitive level, I knew that my brain was different. It kept me from concentrating on one thing at a time and completing tasks in a linear, organized way, but it wasn't all bad. I also had greater mental bandwidth that allowed me to pick up on countless subtleties around me.

This made me very smart in some ways, but totally spaced out in other ways. It was hard to square it. I didn't understand why I was like this and was constantly frustrated that I couldn't get my shit together. Those four screens competed for my attention every minute of the day. I was so busy following all four plotlines. No wonder I was distracted and forgetful! But I was also able to do a lot with what I saw on those four screens.

I often wonder how different my life would have been if I'd been diagnosed with ADHD as a kid, if my parents had thought to seek treatment or even put me on medication. Would I have done better in college? Sure, I bet I would have. I couldn't have done much worse. But would I have had the same successes later on in life too? That I can't say. ADHD is funny. Later on, it helped me drive my business forward in a fanatical, single-minded fashion. But in my home and personal life, it's been much more of a burden.

As it was, I found myself at the University of Miami with no diagnosis, no treatment, and no plan. Honestly, it pains me even to think about it. I was just pathetic. I don't remember going to a single class, although I'm sure I made it to at least a few. But much clearer in my memory are the absolute mess of my dorm room, the potent blended smell of tanning oil and weed, the days spent sleeping, and nights of endless partying.

My roommate was a kid from the Midwest. He didn't know me, and he didn't think I was charming. He couldn't understand why I had so few possessions and could barely function. I had no idea how to take care of myself in the most basic ways. "You could put all of your things in a shoebox and just leave," he said to me in disbelief one day. "Is there something wrong with you?"

I had a few buddies from high school with me in Miami. We were all messed up, but I was by far the worst of us. In high school, we'd tried heavy drugs a few times, but we had mostly stuck to weed. In Miami, drugs were everywhere, and this is where I first fell in love with quaaludes, which we called 714s. Quaaludes are sedatives that were originally used to treat anxiety and insomnia, and they were very popular back then. For a brief window of time, they were legal with a doctor's prescription. That window soon closed when their abuse rate started going through the roof.

Pretty much as soon as we landed in Miami, my buddies and I found a doctor with a reputation for handing prescriptions out easily. Then we quickly made appointments and claimed that we needed those 714s to help us sleep or because we were so stressed out about studying. Then we'd drink excessively, take the 714s, and experience something like euphoria. I felt a warm tingle throughout my body, and all of a sudden, I loved everyone. I saw the mailman coming with my mail and put my arm around him. "I want to be close to you," I slurred, meaning every word.

Because they relax the nervous system and literally slow down the pulse, blood pressure, and heart rate, quaaludes temporarily alleviated my symptoms of ADHD. For the brief thirty minutes to an hour that quaaludes stayed in my system, the screens in my mind went blank. It was heaven, an escape like I had never experienced before. And I was in trouble.

I now know that one of the greatest downsides to a condition like ADHD is the tendency to self-medicate. While most of the time my friends could call it quits after one or two pills and switch to alcohol for the rest of the night, I had no self-control once I started using. I took more and more, searching for that brief escape. But it never came back quite as good, and I was constantly left wanting.

I learned an addict's tricks: taking the pills on an empty stomach so nothing would interfere with the high, and timing them out precisely to keep that high going for as long as possible. Getting loaded was all that mattered. Everything else was a waste of time. It was a singularly focused yet profoundly sad existence.

The one bright spot in my life in Miami was that I could spend more time with my brother John. For the past decade, he had been an elusive, God-like figure that I saw a few times a year, pretty much only on holidays.

The truth is that, while I looked up to him, I hardly knew him. But he had just gotten married and moved to Miami, and now we had a chance to reconnect as brothers.

John was almost thirty by then, and I was more in awe of him than ever. He was always wearing a sharp Pierre Cardin suit, and his gorgeous wife, Toni, was like the princess of the Five Towns. She was from the wealthiest family in town and had grown up on a huge estate. Of course my brother had married her.

John and Toni looked like a movie star couple and lived in a swanky modern condo in Miami. It was decorated in the bright colors, glossy furniture, and modern, geometric shapes that were en vogue in the mid-1970s. One of their Richard Lindner lithographs probably cost more than our dad's textile business earned in a month. It was all so sophisticated and *adult*. I couldn't imagine ever leading a life as grown up and glamorous as theirs.

For the first time in our lives, John and I truly felt like brothers, if not equals. John came out drinking with my buddies and me at bars and clubs all over Miami, but he wasn't into drugs like we were. He was a good-time Charlie, charming everyone and always buying the last round at the bar. I loved being with him, but I'm not sure if he felt the same way. I was using like crazy and often made an ass out of myself. The very nature of quaaludes was that they turned you into a total embarrassment, slurring and drooling and falling over, all with no sense of remorse because you're too blissed out to give a shit about anything else.

One night we were at The Cockpit Lounge, a small, packed club near the Miami airport, and I kept taking pills long after the other guys had stopped. I fell out in the middle of the floor and woke up the next day on John's de Sede leather couch in his pristine living room, wearing his clothes. I had zero recollection of what had happened the night before, but I was mortified knowing that my big brother had to babysit me. That didn't mean it would be the last time, however.

I lasted one year in college. After seeing my grades, my dad called me on the phone in my dorm. He was in his sixties and was getting ready to retire, and he had no patience for my foolishness. "You're cut off," he told me gruffly. "You're not taking school seriously, and I refuse to waste my money. Go get a job." And that was it. I don't recall saying one word in that conversation. What was there to say?

I hung up and looked around my dorm room. It was a disaster. Well, my half of the room, anyway. Clean clothes mingled with dirty ones, because if I actually did a wash, which was rare, I never managed to fold and put my laundry away. Food rotted in the garbage can. Where and when was that garbage even supposed to be emptied? I'd been there for a year and had never learned. I waited to start feeling angry with my dad or disappointed that I had to leave college, but what came over me instead was an intense and unmistakable feeling of relief. Thank goodness this part of my life was over.

Now I can say for sure that my dad did me the biggest favor of my life by yanking my ass out of college. What I needed was to fend for myself and work hard, not an all-expenses-paid, four-year vacation. If I had stayed in college, there's no doubt I would've fallen deeper into the hole of addiction. Not that this isn't exactly what ended up happening, anyway. Some things are truly unavoidable. But at least my father wasn't complicit in my fall. Now, when I see kids go to college and do well, I'm astounded. I wish I could have been like that, but it was simply impossible for me.

I was done with college, but I didn't rush home to Long Island. John had started a company selling home alarm systems called Madden Securities, and he gave me a job as a salesman. I traveled door-to-door selling alarm systems, went to stores all over Miami, put up flyers and stickers, and generally canvassed the whole area. It was so much easier for me to show up to a job and work all day than it had been to try to figure out the in-between moments of college. I have never been afraid of hard work, but some types of work were more manageable for me than others.

We had a little business going at Madden Securities, but it wasn't sustainable. John wasn't really making any money, and we were out drinking and partying every night. The party couldn't go on forever. After about six months, John's wife was pregnant, and he decided to dissolve the security business to get his stockbroker's license. I bet he was glad to get rid of me.

The idea of looking for another job and an apartment in Miami was untenable, so I headed back home to the Five Towns with a shoehorn in my back pocket and moved back in with my mom and dad.

Thanks to my experience at Toulouse, I got a job right away selling shoes at Jildor, a popular shoe store in nearby downtown Cedarhurst. With all three of their sons out on their own, at least temporarily, my parents had sold their house and moved into a small apartment in town. For a while, I slept on a pullout couch in the living room until the building's management company asked my parents to get rid of me.

I was out late every night and came home high, stumbling around and crashing into furniture in the lobby. I could never keep track of my keys, so I often pounded on the door in the middle of the night, needing to be let in. I was an embarrassment, and my parents hated having me there. Now that I think about it, maybe they just used the management company as an excuse to give me the boot. They didn't discipline me or try to straighten me out, and I doubt they would have been able to if they had tried. They just kicked me out and left me to find my way on my own.

So, I convinced my friends Brian Frank and Jeff Melcer from high school to move with me to a little house in Atlantic Beach. Since Atlantic Beach is a popular vacation destination in the summer, we were able to get cheap short-term rentals during the off-season. We went from one short-term rental to another. After a while, Jeff moved out and our old friend Dean Fixler moved in with Brian and me. Our rental houses were always a mess, and so was I. I helped Brian get a job working with me at Jildor, and we worked together all day, got high every night, and tried to meet girls. Most of the time we were unsuccessful.

With no checks and balances on my behavior, my descent into addiction began in earnest. I hadn't fully unraveled yet. At the time, Dean was much worse off than Brian or me, and it got so bad that we eventually told Dean he had to move out. He was always high, damaged the rentals we lived in, and we were worried that one day we'd come home from work and find him dead. We were just kids; we didn't know how to help him. So, we shipped him back to his parents' house, hoping it would motivate him to clean up his act.

In fairness, I was only marginally better off than Dean. During the day, though, I gave my all to my job at Jildor. Unlike Toulouse, which was funky and young, with loud music playing and wild shoes scattered everywhere, Jildor was a pristine, grown-up shoe store selling high-fashion styles. It was neat and organized, the floor always shined, and the entire store smelled like leather. The customers at Jildor were primarily wealthy Jewish women, and working there was a *job*. Eight hours on the floor leaning over a stool, fetching item after item like a waiter often felt like drudgery. But I enjoyed the work.

It probably sounds mundane. Although Jildor was on the fancier side, it was still basically a mom-and-pop shoe store. Not the most exciting place for a creative young person. But I was excited to see that selling shoes could actually be a creative pursuit.

One day, a mother and her adult daughter came into Jildor to buy the daughter a new pair of shoes. The mom had no intention of buying shoes for herself, but when she mentioned that she worked at the bank in town, I steered her toward some new pumps we'd just gotten in. "I can't wait to come into the bank and see you wearing these," I told her as I boxed them up alongside a pair of boots for her daughter. "They're going to look great." Both women left the store visibly delighted by their new shoes. These moments were thrilling and proved that I had something to offer.

I was naturally a good seller, but I improved on these skills with the help of Jildor's owner, Jack Bienenfeld. I would not be where I am today if I hadn't spent those two years learning from Jack and his business. Jack was an elegant man in his fifties with excellent posture and white hair who was as fastidious about his own appearance as he was about how the store was maintained. As the owner, he was somewhat removed. He came down to the floor from his office upstairs about once a week. Although he wasn't present on a daily basis, Jack's principles suffused the atmosphere. Everyone knew to keep the store immaculate at all times, with every dust bunny swept away and each shoe display perfectly aligned.

One day Jack came down and noticed that the window was smudged. He turned to us in disbelief and anger. "What the hell is this?" he asked us, pointing at the window. "Where is your sense of pride?" We learned to clean the glass every hour on the hour, and the smell of Windex soon competed with the leather in the air.

But the most important thing was that the bulbs lighting up the store name outside on the marquee were always shining. If one of those bulbs went out and wasn't replaced within seconds, it was the absolute end of the world, equivalent to a death in the family. You could not let Jack see the marquee like that. Your life almost literally depended on it.

The store's appearance reflected Jack's pride in his business, and I took this philosophy with me into my own retail stores. To this day, if I see a store with a light bulb out, I think, *they don't give a shit*. And I go ballistic if there is a carton of shoes sitting on the floor or a messy shoe display in a Steve Madden store.

Most of all, I learned from Jack the importance of making sure that everyone who works in a store is wearing items that are sold there. What kind of message does it send if you go into a shoe store and the salespeople are wearing shoes from a brand that store doesn't carry?

Recently, I went into the little store at my gym where they sell workout clothes and gear. The young woman working at the store was wearing a cute pair of leggings. I asked her, "Where did you get those?"

She smiled at me. "Forever 21," she said innocently. *Unbelievable!* They sell leggings at that store. How can they stand for that? To be clear, I don't blame the salesclerk. Clearly, they're not giving their staff a big enough discount. To me, it's worth it to give shoes and accessories to staff members for free or at a huge discount so they are out there wearing and representing the brand.

At Steve Madden, salespeople are not allowed on the floor if they are not wearing our shoes. Period. I spend a lot of time in our retail stores, and whenever I see salespeople in another brand of shoes, I walk right over and tell them, "Get off the floor." It may sound harsh, but it all comes down to pride. That's what I learned from Jack.

Most of the staff at Jildor were terrified of Jack, but he took a liking to me and Brian and the other young guys who worked on the floor. He taught us how to hustle and sell, two things that always came naturally to me. If a woman asked to see one shoe in her size, Jack taught us to bring her another, similar style as well. That woman came in to buy something, so give her every opportunity to find the right thing. I was learning new steps to the dance I'd started at Toulouse and have continued choreographing to this day.

My fundamentals today all came from those two years working the floor at Jildor. But nobody around me thought that job would lead me anywhere. Besides Brian, my friends were all taking the train into the city to work in the Garment District or on Wall Street like our fathers, while I just rode my bike over to Jildor. They made fun of me for working at a shoe store like a high school kid, but I loved it. In the back of my mind, I hoped it would somehow lead to a real career.

Even then, I took a keen interest in the design of the shoes and what made one shoe sell over another. For women, pumps were very big in those days. The most sought-after brand was Charles Jourdan, which were the Louboutins of their time. The shoes came in these gorgeous red boxes and, on Long Island, they were exclusive to Jildor. It was thrilling to open the cases and pull out those coveted red boxes.

Twice a year, Jack would put the Charles Jourdans on sale at half price. Now, stores are always having sales. But back then, we'd sell the whole season at full price and then, when the next season's shoes came in, we would have a big sale. This was long before online shopping, and people would come from all over the metropolitan area just for the sale.

Jack put up ropes like it was a movie premiere, and women lined up down the street before opening to get into the store. As soon as the doors opened . . . *charge!* Women poured in, creating a frenzy as they ran toward the table of Jourdans. Years later, I put up ropes for our grand opening of Steve Madden's first retail store as a tip of the hat to Jack. Without Jildor, there would be no Steve Madden.

After two years on the floor, I was ready to get out and try something new. Lance from Toulouse had started a little wholesale shoe business called L. J. Simone at around the same time that I'd started working at Jildor. L. J. Simone was one of the first real junior brands that made shoes specifically for women under thirty. Jack had wanted to sell them at Jildor, but Lance refused since he sold them at Toulouse right around the corner. I wandered into Toulouse at one point to check out the shoes. They had lots of European-looking wooden clogs with funky details like rivets and stacked heels, and I thought they were pretty cool.

Not long after, Lance called and asked me to come and work for him. L. J. Simone was a tiny company. It was just Lance; his partners, Jay and Larry; and a few other guys, but they were making some noise, and they needed someone to sell their shoes to stores. I jumped at the chance without thinking about the fact that I had no idea how to do this. Nobody taught me. I just packed up a sample bag with the current line and spent my days traveling to every shoe store in the tristate area to try to sell them our shoes.

There was only one problem: I was twenty-two years old, but I didn't have a driver's license. It wasn't that I had never learned to drive. I had gotten my license at sixteen, but I'd lost it right around the time I started working at L. J. Simone because I had gotten so many DUIs. On the island we called them *deewees*. Not only was I a bad driver to begin with, but I'm ashamed to say that I was also high pretty much all the time, even when I was driving.

During the years I worked at Jildor, I crashed more cars than I could remember, and I got pulled over constantly. Eventually my driving record was such a disgrace that my license was taken away. But I needed to get around to sell shoes for L. J. Simone, and I wasn't going to let a few deewees stop me.

I didn't have a car of my own, so I borrowed cars from friends, rented cars when a company would let me, and did whatever I had to do to sell those shoes. To get around the city, I could use the Long Island Rail Road and the subway. But to go out to Connecticut and Westchester County, I had to rent a car. Many times, I crashed those cars too.

One of the cars I borrowed belonged to my old friend Danny Porush. We had stayed in touch since high school, and Danny was now at college in Boston. He had a car, and I convinced him to let me borrow it for a while. I actually gave him money for each day I had it, like a real rental. One day, I pulled up in front of Macy's in Herald Square and left the driver's-side door open for a minute as I got my sample bag out of the trunk. Just before I headed back around to close the door . . . *bam*! A truck drove into the door and tore it right off.

This was the one time an accident actually wasn't my fault, but of course Danny had no reason to believe that. He was furious, but not nearly as angry as his father, who tried to sue me even after I offered to pay for the car repair. Eventually his dad backed down, but after that, Danny and I didn't speak again for several years.

I was a disaster, and the predominance of drugs definitely didn't help. It was New York City in the early 1980s, and drugs were everywhere, particularly cocaine. Some of my friends preferred coke to quaaludes, so I did coke with them once in a while on top of quaaludes and plenty of booze.

Cocaine is a horrible drug. Every time I took it, I'd feel terrible and grind my teeth, but I'd still keep taking more. It made me paranoid, thinking that people were after me. Many times, I'd lock myself in my apartment, high on cocaine, and push the love seat and sofa against the door. I thought the police were coming any minute to arrest me.

The next day, I'd make the rounds to shoe stores shaking because I'd used so much the night before. But as soon as I was done working for the day, I'd start using again. The drugs had complete and total control over me.

I put the same zeal into my work as I did into getting high. I wasn't a weekend warrior; I was a full-time barbarian. At L. J. Simone I had the opportunity to learn every aspect of the wholesale business, from designing shoes to selling shoes to shipping shoes. Jay was the operating boss, and he was a year younger than me. He was a tough workaholic who taught me the guts of the business, and I looked up to him. We made a lot of wedges, platforms, and flats, which were becoming a big deal in women's shoes. Lance was in charge of design, but I'd go to our little factory on Twenty-Fifth Street in Manhattan and fiddle around with the pattern maker. "The bottom of that shoe," I said, rummaging through some samples. "What if you put the upper from this other one on there?"

The designs I came up with were effective, and I quickly found that I had a knack for knowing what women wanted to buy. But even then, I never saw a shoe as just a product the way a full-time designer might. I could fast-forward in my mind all the way to the end of the process, the whole thing playing out on the four screens in my mind: how much it would cost to make, how to price it, how to place it in the market so a lot of women could afford to buy it, and how to do it all in a way that made money. Creativity with no bottom line was, and still is, boring to me, whether it's music or art or shoes.

I took many lessons from L. J. Simone with me when I started Steve Madden. One that made the biggest difference was knowing how to make a splash at shoe shows. Every season, brands would put their next line of shoes on display in hotel rooms, and buyers from shoe stores around the country would come to look at the shoes and place their orders. This is how we sold to stores that I couldn't physically travel to with my sample bag.

Before L. J. Simone came around, these shows were incredibly old-fashioned and boring. Sales guys from every shoe brand would just sit around in their hotel rooms reading the newspaper and waiting for someone to come in and place an order. At L. J. Simone, we did it differently. They took out a big suite at the hotel where the show was held, put out food and champagne, blasted music, and made the place feel like a giant party. We even packed the house with employees and friends to make it feel like we were the hot, in-demand brand. This created a lot of buzz. And, indeed, it *was* a party. Most of the time I'd been up snorting coke and taking pills the entire night before.

I'd been at L. J. Simone for a couple years when I finally moved from Long Island into the city, to an apartment on Mercer Street in the Village. Greenwich Village in the 1980s was everything I had imagined when I was a little boy taking the train in with my dad. It was an explosion of color and noise and music and drugs and people of every type and shade who were just a little bit demented. I fit right in.

For the next several years, I continued to work like a lunatic all day and then get blasted at night. We blew it up at L. J. Simone and created quite a successful little business, but it's painful to think about the crashed cars, the messy living conditions, and the many places I fell out: naked in the hallway of my apartment building, at countless clubs and restaurants and diners, even on top of a girl I'd brought home from one of them.

Drugs diminished me as a person. The full field of vision I'd always had access to was narrowed, and my charm and intellect were squashed by this beast that completely controlled me. As I relive it, I honestly can't imagine how I survived.

By then I had started to make a little bit of money with L. J. Simone, which was like hot water for the hurricane of my addiction. I fell down all the time and woke up with cuts and bruises covering my body, so I started wearing extra layers of clothing for padding. At one point, I bought a sunlamp and set it up on the floor of my apartment. Don't ask me why I bought a sunlamp—it was just one of my random ideas. When I woke up in the morning, it was completely flattened, like in a cartoon, and my ribs hurt so bad that I had to hold onto the wall to walk.

The extra clothes clearly weren't cutting it. I had seen a famous *Saturday Night Live* bit that advertised The William Holden Drinking Helmet. Holden, a famous actor and alcoholic, had died after slipping on a rug and hitting his head on a table on his way down. In one of my worst moments, I actually went out and bought a helmet because I was worried that something similar might happen to me.

As my addiction got worse, so did my relationship with the guys at L. J. Simone. I'm pretty sure that was no coincidence. While I gave them my all, I was also high most of the time, and I'm sure I embarrassed the company on more occasions than I can remember. As much as Jay taught me what to do when I started my own company, he also taught me what not to do. He was a great shoe man with two major flaws: One, he could not let go and allow other people to be the boss. And two, he wasn't great at paying his bills. My perception was that he liked having some level of control over his salespeople when he owed them money, but I saw how this hurt him in the long run.

From the moment I started Steve Madden, I've always brought people in and given them a stake in the company. It helps them feel ownership and begets loyalty from talented people who would otherwise move on and eventually get another job. I've made a lot of millionaires along the way. I'm proud of that. And I'm proud of the fact that almost all of our very first employees are still with the company.

Jay wasn't like that. While he paid me fairly for my work, he always made it clear that he was the boss and I was an employee. There was no way for me to grow, no sense of real partnership. That was his prerogative, but at the time, it really pissed me off. Now I realize that it might have been me. I wasn't doing myself any favors with my behavior.

Toward the end of my eight-year run with L. J. Simone, I was at Macy's on yet another sales call. I was wasted, as usual, slurring my words as I weaved my way across the store. I must have passed out briefly, because all I remember is coming to lying on the ground with an entire rack of dresses on top of me.

The buyer at Macy's was a nice guy who I'd known for a while, and he got me outside and into a cab. I sat there in the back seat with the cabbie yelling at me, "Where do you want to go?" For several minutes, I could not for the life of me remember where I lived.

The next day, I walked into the L. J. Simone offices near the factory on Twenty-Fifth Street and heard Jay call out, asking me to come into his office. "Steve, we have to talk," he said sternly. "I keep getting reports about your behavior. I need you to clean up your act, or you can't be out there representing this company."

The thing is, Jay was absolutely right. I was a goddamned mess. That's painfully clear to me now, but at the time, I hated him. Beyond my tension with Jay, though, I knew that I had outgrown L. J. Simone. I had learned all that I could learn from them and was starting to realize that I didn't need them anymore. I could do this on my own. So, I left. Lance was pissed. Jay was relieved. But I had given them eight years of my life, and it was time for me to move on.

In my intoxicated state, however, I wasn't ready to be completely independent. Instead, I found two partners: Alfie, a designer who owned a shoe factory, and Steven, a jobber who sold shoes people didn't want to outlet stores. We each put in a little bit of money and formed the company Soulier, the French word for shoe. It sounds pretentious as hell now, but at the time people loved the name.

Soulier started out strong. I had a good sense of what kind of shoes young women wanted to wear and focused on making the same kind of hip, trendy shoes I'd been selling at L. J. Simone for years. Our first line had these color-blocked boots that were a huge hit and were ahead of their time. We also sold these cool pumps that were covered in jewels. At our first shoe show in June 1988, Nordstrom placed a huge order, and we were ecstatic. The shoes sold well throughout the summer, but by November the line had stopped selling, and the stores were asking us what was next for Soulier.

I can't put my finger on the exact reason, but we never managed to follow up that first line with anything decent. We just burned out. I learned the valuable lesson then that, no matter how well things are going in business, you can never let yourself coast. You've got to keep moving and pushing forward, always looking ahead and around corners for potential problems and opportunities.

As it was, Alfie and Steven started fighting about money, and my descent into addiction became a crash-and-burn scenario. Any addict will tell you that he has to hit bottom, and then another bottom, and then another, before making any changes. For me, it was when the drugs started to impact my work in a big way.

Soulier wasn't selling, I was broke, my partners were fighting, and my drug use had gotten so bad that I stopped going out at night because I knew something terrible would probably happen—I'd end up in a hospital, in jail, or dead. So, I just stayed home and got wasted on my couch, alone.

One night, I was alone in my apartment, high as usual. I had cinder blocks in the living room with books stacked on top of them. Despite everything, I was still an avid reader. Books and drugs were my favorite escapes. I was thrashing around the room doing God knows what when the cinder blocks collapsed, and the books came tumbling down.

This may sound strange. It was not nearly as dramatic a rock bottom as some addicts experience, but for me, this was the final straw. I looked around my messy, shitty apartment with the books everywhere and thought, *What else can go wrong?* Things had been so bad for so long, and I guess the time was right or I was finally miserable enough to actually do something about it.

03
COUNTER

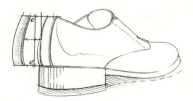

counter • a piece of material forming the back of a shoe to give
support and stiffen the material at the back of the heel.

O n January 10, 1989, I forced myself into a meeting on Perry Street in Greenwich Village. I'd walked by that storefront dozens of times and often thought about going in, but this time I knew that I really had no choice. If I didn't change something, I wouldn't be around much longer.

If you were at that meeting, you might have noticed that I looked straitlaced and conservative compared to the other people filling the room. Back then, I looked like a member of the Young Republican Club with my penny loafers, khaki pants, and Lacoste button-downs. I was already losing my hair and, embarrassingly, kept a long ponytail in the back. But inside I felt like just as much of an outcast or rebel as everyone else. That's often how things were for me in the Village. Today it's full of high-end chain stores and yoga moms, but historically it was a haven for avant-garde artists, bohemians, and the majority of New York City's gay community.

That meeting contained much of the same stew: artists, playwrights, actors, and a few blue-collar guys thrown in for good measure. It was an interesting mix of people, for sure, but there was no one in there quite like me. Or so I thought. At first, I noticed all the ways I was different from these folks. But the very magic of the program is that it forces you to see that you're not really any different, and that means you're not alone.

I sat in that little storefront sipping coffee with my head hung slightly forward as I listened to the people around me tell their stories. At the time, I was very conservative in my beliefs as well as in my looks. I held no hatred for anyone, but I trended right politically. My daddy was a big right-winger way before it was fashionable, and at that point I hadn't really questioned his way of thinking. I have since learned better. Prison in particular provided quite a reeducation, and my politics eventually swung a full 180 degrees. But this change started, albeit gradually, in that very first meeting. I recognized that the other people in that room weren't only more like me than they seemed, but in many ways, they were *exactly* like me. Their stories were my story, and I was no better or worse than any of them.

On my right sat a woman named International Chrysis who was a local celebrity and one of the great, original transgender entertainers who epitomized the beauty and glamour of the 1980s downtown club scene. She toured nightclubs performing her revues, *Jesus Chrysis Superstar* and *The Last Temptation of Chrysis,* and had been Salvador Dali's protégée.

Chrysis, as we called her, showed up to meetings wearing floor-length, sequined gowns with long trains, and always had a group of guys who were like her sycophants trailing behind her, carrying the train of her dress. I learned later that she had been in recovery for a long time and helped many others along the way. Her exterior was over the top, but on the inside, she was humble and generous. I was the exact opposite. On the outside, I appeared normal, maybe even boring. But I took everything to excess.

As soon as she learned it was my first meeting, Chrysis took a keen interest in me. "You just have to take it one day at a time, sweetie," she said.

On my other side sat an older Italian guy named Guido who owned a small ice cream shop around the corner. He turned to us. "Acceptance is the answer," he said, nodding. "Be where your feet are."

The two of them continued going back and forth, building me up little by little with the wisdom of the program. Somehow, amazingly, it worked. I felt more hopeful than I had in as long as I could remember. It sounds impossible to me now, but in that moment, it seemed like I had been waiting my whole life to hear exactly what they were saying.

Addiction is a lifelong battle; one I still fight every single day. Along the way, I've had slips both big and small. But that day and for the next several years, the urge to use was lifted from me. It was simply gone, like magic. I didn't take it for granted. I worked the system, like we say, going to meetings every single day, twice a day at first.

The people I met in recovery quickly became my closest friends. We've lost a few soldiers along the way, but many of them are still my dear friends. We were like a family of misfits of all ages, races, and persuasions. There was Eddie Lama, a tough street guy from Brooklyn with the heart of a poet who was starting out in the construction business after a stint in prison; Peter Torres, a handsome and charismatic Puerto Rican artist who had a great combination of creativity and swag; and Harry Koutoukas, a legendary off-Broadway playwright.

A group of us would meet every morning for coffee at a little café called Lanciani, and then we'd go to a meeting. Afterward, we'd hang out on Perry Street smoking our Marlboros and commiserating about our lives. There was a mailbox right outside that we used as a makeshift coffee table slash altar for those post-meeting sessions that came to be as essential to my sobriety and my sanity as the program itself.

As soon as I got clean, my head was clear enough to finally move my professional life forward. Soulier had simply frayed apart at the seams. It was disappointing, but I was ready to move on when two guys I knew from my days at L. J. Simone approached me.

Nick and Sal were two older Italian men who had been successful in the shoe business separately for decades. Sal owned a broken-down shoe factory way out in East New York, Brooklyn. He was a real character who loved nothing more than sitting at his decrepit desk in that factory with the suffocating machinery noise all around him. Nick was a shoemaker who was famous for going on his band saw and making tremendous platform shoes. When he was done, he'd have sawdust all over his face.

These guys were old school, and they knew they needed someone younger to work with them if they were going to make a go of starting a new business. That's where I came in. I loved the idea of pairing their old-school work ethic with my forward-thinking designs and creativity. Nick and Sal had partnered up, and they came to me with an offer to go into business together: They would own the business, and I would design and sell the shoes under my name in exchange for a 10 percent royalty.

In other words, I owned the brand, and they owned the business. This meant I had to cover all the expenses that went along with designing and selling the shoes out of my 10 percent, and they'd handle everything else. That 10 percent may not seem like much. If we shipped thirty thousand dollars' worth of shoes, I'd get three thousand. But it was a good way to start a business when I didn't have any money. I scraped together the sum total of eleven hundred dollars I had in savings and used that to fund my side of the business until our first invoices came in.

Before we got started, I wasn't sure what to name the new brand. Sal and Nick had said we could use my name or whatever moniker I chose, and I wondered if I should use something like Soulier that sounded like a real shoe brand. After a meeting one morning, I asked Eddie what he thought as we smoked our cigarettes, resting our coffee cups on the mailbox that stood between us.

"Steve, it's a no-brainer," he said right away in his thick Brooklyn accent. "I bet those shoes will be as unique and crazy as you are. Could it be any other name but yours?"

I laughed. "I guess not," I said, and Steve Madden the brand, but not the business, was born.

Back then, though, there was really no such thing as branding. You made a shoe, put a label on it, and sold it to stores. Boom. But I did take some time to think about the labels that went inside my shoes. Like Eddie said, I already knew that I wanted to make shoes that were funky and unique, so I saw the label as an opportunity to make them seem like a safe bet.

I was always struck by the fact that male comedians of the time often wore a nice suit, even if their material was raunchy or controversial. I realized that the suit was there to put audiences at ease so they would be open to hearing his most outlandish jokes. I wanted to do the same thing with my shoes. So, I created a very straight, plain logo bearing my name to give the shoes an air of gravitas. These are the same labels we use in all Steve Madden shoes today.

My sobriety was a good fit for this new start. Finally, I had a clear mind and the ferocious energy I needed to focus completely on designing and selling shoes. Free from the limitations of a boss calling the shots, I felt I could finally reach my potential.

The first shoe we made for Steve Madden was a flat, over-the-knee boot in a style that was really hot at the time, and we followed those up with some clogs. I already knew from tinkering around at L. J. Simone and Soulier that I had a knack for making shoes that women wanted to buy, ones that were affordable and stylish and easy to wear.

It was an exciting time, but I had no salary or safety net. I could only eat if I sold shoes. That was a pretty big motivator. It wasn't like I could call my parents for help if I didn't make the rent one month. They had retired by then and moved down to Florida, and my dad had been diagnosed with a heart condition that he controlled with medication. I only saw my family a few times a year, mostly during holidays. It felt good to have this healthy distance between us. But they'd never been the kind of parents to bail me out.

I couldn't afford to hire anyone, but once again I needed a driver to get around town and sell shoes. Yes, I was sober, but I still didn't have a license, and I knew better now than to mess around with illegally renting cars or borrowing from friends. One morning, I was leaving my apartment on my way to my regular meeting when I saw my building's night-shift doorman, David Cristobal, getting into a 1985 red Nissan Sentra. It wasn't pretty, but it was a car.

David had seen me at my worst: passed out and falling down countless times. He was the one who'd had to let me in when I'd somehow locked myself out of my apartment buck-naked. He was the one who'd come upstairs to help when I'd passed out, and the girl in my apartment had thought I was dead. He was a decent, solid guy who still treated me kindly after all of that, and, hey, he had a car. David agreed to be my driver during the day and officially became my first hire.

I paid David in cash every day to avoid ever being in debt or having to pay a bill. This is a small thing that I believe was germane to my early success. Even after I hired more staff, until I had someone else handling our finances, I paid each of them at the end of the day by peeling a few bills off of the roll of cash I kept in my pocket.

My whole life, I've been horrible at paying bills. And I was terrified of having to keep track of invoices and ending up owing people money. When you're in the early days of starting a business, you can find yourself upside down so easily, and this can keep you from ever getting off the ground. Cash flow is a constant struggle for every entrepreneur. If you earn one nickel less than you owe, it can all fall apart. By paying everyone in cash by the day, I avoided this fate. It also kept the people working for me happy, and their loyalty was critical as I was getting the business started.

Soon, I developed a little routine: breakfast at Lanciani, followed by a meeting. Then I'd climb into the little Nissan Sentra and say, "OK, David, let's make another day." We drove to store after store after store. When David pulled up outside, I'd get my two bags of sample shoes out of the trunk and go inside to meet with buyers. Meanwhile, David double-parked or circled around the block for an hour to avoid getting a parking ticket. He still got plenty, by the way.

One day, we were still downtown when I screamed at David to pull over. A young woman on the sidewalk had caught my eye. Actually, it was her shoes that I'd noticed: a pair of flat-heeled boots with fringe along the side. "Hey there." I approached her after getting out of the car. "I love your shoes. Where did you get them?"

She smiled at me, and I realized that she thought I was hitting on her, which was not the case at all. "This little store on Eighth Street," she said. I wasn't surprised. That block of Manhattan was lined with shoe stores back then. But I didn't want to risk going there and not being able to find those exact boots. I needed to take them back to the factory and disman- tle them so I could get a sense of how to tweak the style and make them my own.

"I'll tell you what," I said. "I'll drive you down to Eighth Street and buy you any pair of shoes you want if you give me those." She looked at me like I was crazy, and I held my hands up in mock surrender. "I make shoes," I told her. "I promise I'm not a creep. Look, I have a driver here. We'll head right over to Eighth Street. It will only take a few minutes."

This sort of interaction happened all the time. Whenever I wasn't driving around with David, I was sitting in the shoe department at Macy's or Nordstrom, watching women buy shoes. I wanted to see how they re- sponded to each style they tried on, which pair they ended up buying, and why. If I spotted a woman wearing a pair of shoes I loved, I'd offer to buy them off of her and replace them with any pair in the store.

My pores were always open, and I got my inspiration from everything around me. This included other shoes, music, fashion, and even the art I'd sometimes stop to look at when I was down in SoHo. My energy was totally focused on product and sales. One was meaningless without the other. I wasn't interested in creating a great product that nobody bought or a shitty product that flew off the shelves. The product had to be right *and* make money for me to consider it a success. This has never changed in the thirty years since.

When we were in the car, I was admiring a shoe we'd made, feeling it in my hands and smelling the leather. The front seat of David's car was littered with shoes. Whichever one I was the most excited about at the moment sat in the place of honor right on the dashboard.

That Sentra was our office. Besides shoes, it was full of the notebooks I used to write down orders by hand and keep track of which shoes needed to be shipped where. The car had no air-conditioning, and traffic was always awful in and around the city. The screens in my mind blasted thoughts and ideas at me nonstop, and my environment couldn't keep up. I lost my temper all the time, and David often got the worst of it. When it was hot in the car, I screamed at him about the lack of air-conditioning. When we got stuck in traffic, I ordered him to pull an illegal U-turn with cars flying at us in the opposite direction. For his part, David was always calm and steady. He just kept driving, no matter what I threw at him, literally or figuratively.

One time, we got stuck on the Brooklyn Queens Expressway for more than an hour in bumper-to-bumper traffic, and I thought I was going to lose my goddamn mind. I was late to one sales call and had missed another. Finally, I jumped out of the car and started directing other cars to move this way and that to make an opening for us. A few cars nearly hit me, but I couldn't believe how many of them actually listened to me and moved over to make room for us. This was maybe the one time David saw how nuts I really was. I could hear him yelling at me from the Sentra, "Steve, come back!"

I just ignored him. We *had* to get out of there. Finally, the traffic started really moving, and I ran back to the Sentra, darting around cars as they picked up speed all around me. "Let's go!" I shouted at David as soon as I got back in the car.

Yes, I was sober, but I was still the same asshole as always with no patience and ADHD. I'm not proud of it, but this book is so full of things I'm not proud of that this one hardly ranks. I was maniacally driven to succeed. This made me volatile and restless. I had learned my lesson with Soulier, and I knew I couldn't stop moving for one moment—traffic, rationality, or people's feelings be damned.

Luckily, I met another person in recovery who calmed me somewhat, at least when we were together. Paula was a plucky, intelligent brunette who worked in show business and was newly sober too. When we met, I wasn't used to dating a woman who was funnier than me. Well, Paula was far funnier and cleverer and cooler than me, and I loved it. Whenever I wasn't working, we would bop around the Village together, and she taught me so much about the city. I had been living there for a few years already, but I still felt very much like a country boy from the Five Towns. Paula was a real New Yorker who had grown up in Greenwich Village. She knew every hip store and shop owner and had a downtown aesthetic that had a tremendous influence on me and certainly impacted the early designs of my shoes.

In 1989, there were still very few companies catering to teenagers, but this new generation had a look that was all their own. Generation X was dubbed the "slacker generation" because they were so disaffected. This was the first generation of kids to see their parents divorcing in big numbers. These kids were often left to their own devices because of the rise in both single parents and dual-income families. Their resulting cynicism was reflected in their art, music, and fashion. On top of that, the late 1980s was the golden age of hip-hop, and it overlapped briefly with the birth of grunge. This led to a unique aesthetic that most shoe designers were ether unwilling or unable to incorporate into their designs.

This wasn't my generation. I was already in my early thirties, and my designs were influenced as much by the styles that had dominated during my own teenage years as the current trends. When I was starting out, I thought women my age would love my shoes. And as soon as I started designing as Steve Madden, I did get a fabulous reaction, but I got it from much younger girls than I ever expected. These girls had been abandoned by much of the fashion industry, which was focused on making products for women their mothers' age. The popular shoe brands were still the same ones I'd sold a decade earlier at Jildor. Teen girls rightfully wanted something of their own to distinguish themselves from the older generation.

As soon as I recognized this opportunity, I gladly stepped into it. Young entrepreneurs today would call this "white space mapping." Sure, that sounds good. But I simply think of it as being an opportunist. More than anything else, I've excelled at cracking open a window and jumping through before it closed again. As soon as I saw how ill served teenagers were by most shoe brands and how strongly they responded to my shoes, I headed wholeheartedly down the path of designing specifically for teenaged girls.

To do this as effectively as possible, I needed a designer to work with me. Paula had a coworker named John whose wife, Miranda Morrison, was a talented young shoe designer. I hired her to work for me, and we designed shoes in collaboration. Miranda was a polished, highly educated, young British woman with short, curly hair who spoke very properly and dressed in pressed button-down blouses and skirts. She had just had a baby who she brought with her to work every day.

Miranda and I would meet at Sal's factory in Brooklyn, which was a horrible, inner-city getup, and sit there for hours sketching out designs. I was always struck by the contrast between our decrepit surroundings and Miranda's entire being, between her innocent baby and her own fresh appearance. But she was a good sport, and we got along well. Sitting around the drafting table in the factory, I'd tell her, "I want to do a new mule," or, "How about a platform clog?" She'd start sketching, and together we'd tweak the style until we had something we both liked and that we knew our customers would love.

We were very much a young startup grasping at every opportunity and barely scraping by. Unless there's outside funding, cash flow is the biggest issue for any entrepreneur. Our early shoes were doing well, but I was still living hand to mouth.

Within the first few months of our arrangement, Sal and Nick started being late with my payments, and I needed those commissions to pay David and Miranda, not to mention my own rent. I lived with the knowledge that I was one late payment away from losing everything, and I carried this fear with me long after it was no longer true.

Soon, Miranda left to start her own company with a friend of hers named Kari Sigerson, which they called Sigerson Morrison. They made beautiful high-end designer shoes and went on to become incredibly successful. One year after we opened our first Steve Madden store in SoHo, they opened theirs right around the corner. We were never direct competitors since Sigerson Morrison was selling to a different market, and I loved seeing Miranda's success. In 2012, after they sold their company, I hired both Miranda and Kari to design shoes for Steve Madden.

Back then, my life was full to bursting between work, spending time with Paula, and going to meetings. I liked it that way. In my spare moments, I tried to give back, one of the tenets of the program. I had stayed in touch with Dean, my old roommate from Atlantic Beach. He was still using and was in bad shape. After I had been clean for about a year, I was able to convince Dean to come to a meeting with me, and I was proud of him when he finally got clean.

Dean was now working for our old high school friend Danny Porush. Danny and I hadn't really spoken since the incident with his father's car, but Dean told me all about the Long Island brokerage firm Danny was running called Stratton Oakmont. "It's unbelievable," Dean told me one morning after a meeting. "These guys are raking in the dough. And you would love this guy Jordan Belfort, Danny's partner. He's like a genius or something. What they're doing is incredible."

Jordan Belfort's aura was so strong that I felt it long before I ever met him. To hear Dean talk, Belfort was some kind of stock wunderkind or god or both. He was still in his twenties at that point, but there was no end to the stories about how smart and inspiring Belfort was. And the proof was right there. Stratton was famous for hiring high school dropouts and other degenerates and turning them into millionaires using Belfort's hard-core sales tactics to push shitty stocks on unsuspecting clients. Sure enough, Dean started showing up to meetings wearing nicer and nicer suits and driving increasingly expensive cars.

Dean and I and some of our friends from the program started playing together in a sober basketball league. This was my first time playing any sort of sport since high school. All that had gone out the window in college when my addiction really took hold. Even though I still wasn't very good, I enjoyed playing basketball with my friends, and it was a healthy outlet for some of my restlessness and irascibility.

One night, Danny showed up to one of our games to cheer Dean on. Danny had always been a regular guy who guzzled six-packs in North Woodmere Park. Now he walked into the basketball game wearing a sharp, custom-tailored suit with a Rolex peeking out from under his left cuff. It was clear that everything I'd been hearing about Jordan Belfort was true.

Danny and I reconnected at that basketball game, the incident with his car long behind us, and he started selling me on Stratton pretty much right away. At first, he kept telling me what a genius Jordan Belfort was. Then, not long after, Danny and I met for dinner at a steakhouse on Second Avenue, and he started pitching me in sincerity over bloody steak tartar and thick-cut fries.

"I've known you my whole life," Danny told me, "and I think you're really talented. We can raise money for you now. Probably six hundred grand. And eventually we'll take your company public. Then you'd get millions."

Now, six hundred grand is a lot of money. Back then, it was even more. And for someone like me who had so little, it would be life changing. But in that moment, I just laughed at Danny. I didn't think he could really get me that much money, but I played along anyway, sensing an opportunity. I didn't know how they had become so successful, but it was obvious to me that there was something interesting going on at Stratton Oakmont. Like I said, I am an opportunist. I may not be the most strategic thinker in the world, but if I get an inkling of something, I'm there. And, for better or worse, that was certainly the case with Stratton.

Soon after that, I went to the Stratton Oakmont offices in Lake Success, Long Island, and met Jordan Belfort for the first time. To put it simply, he lived up to his billing. Jordan was like no one else I had ever met before or since. And despite everything that happened between us after that first meeting, I will tell you without hesitation that he became one of the most influential people in my life.

As I was working on this book, I listened to Michael Cohen, Donald Trump's lawyer, talking about how he got sucked into working for this intimidating, swaggy guy who he knew was breaking the law and acting immorally. And the first thing I thought of as I listened was what it was like to be around Jordan Belfort. He was magnetic. Not only was he incredibly good-looking, but he was also intelligent and charismatic and had a way of talking to you that made it seem like anything was possible.

At the same time, Jordan had an air about him that made you sit up straight. Everyone wanted to please him, and I understood right away how he had amassed these disciples. Jordan was physically small—something he was sensitive about—but his energy and aura more than compensated for his size. As soon as we met, he started selling me on the idea of working together, and he was quite a seller.

In his office, he stared into my eyes. His were piercing and blue. "Danny tells me you're a genius," he said, pointing at me with his finger, "and I can see it. You're an innovator, an artist, not just some asshole making shoes, but a real, honest-to-God, Great American Cobbler."

Jordan paused to look out the window as if contemplating how unbelievable the future was going to be. Then he returned his gaze to me. "Our firm wants to invest in you," he said. "We believe in you so much that we're going to give you five hundred thousand dollars to bring your company to the next level. And when you're ready, we'll take you public and make you a multi-fucking-millionaire." Another pause. "I'm telling you, Cobbler, with your talent and my highly trained, ferocious sales force out there, together we'll be unstoppable." Jordan gestured outside of his office to his team of five hundred or so brokers, each of them screaming obscenities into the phone. His pride was palpable.

After that meeting, I did my research, asking around to find out what exactly was going on over there and how they were making so much dough. It didn't take much prodding to figure it out. Stratton Oakmont was a classic pump-and-dump stock company. They would take crappy companies public, artificially jack up the stock price, and then sell off their shares at a huge profit. Hence the name: pump (inflate) and dump (sell). Every day, Jordan hyped his team of brokers up like rabid dogs before they got on the phone and used scripts Jordan had written to intimidate people into buying shitty stocks at inflated prices.

In the late 1980s and early '90s, the times were ripe for firms like this to bloom. Stratton was simply the most effective and infamous of the lot. They called it the "boiler room era" of brokerage houses because interest rates, which had been insanely high throughout most of the 1980s, were finally starting to come down. While those rates were high, venture capital funding had pretty much all dried up, so for the first time the markets started allowing initial public offerings (IPOs) on companies and even ideas that were still unproven. For the next decade or so, tons of IPOs hit the market for companies that were basically put together with spit and paste.

The amazing thing was that once their clients inevitably lost money on these shitty stocks, the Strattonites, as Jordan called them, somehow convinced them to invest in a "new, hot company" to earn back that money instead of calling it quits. It didn't matter that this new company was just as lousy a bet as the first one.

Steve Madden fit that profile. It was hardly even a company at that point, but that wasn't a problem at all for the guys at Stratton. If anything, it's probably why they were so interested in working with me. Jordan and Danny came out to the dilapidated factory in Brooklyn in their stretch limo to look at my shoes and pumped me full of praise when they saw my designs. They claimed that they were doing their due diligence, but I knew they would have taken a hot dog stand public if they could make money at it. The limo and the site visit, like so much of what they did, were just for show.

In the meantime, though, I knew these guys could help me make money in another way: by bringing me in on their other deals as what's called a flipper. In this role, I would buy shares of a company they were taking public before the IPO, and then sell those shares on the opening as soon as the stock prices were nice and inflated. In other words, I was pumping and dumping right alongside them, aiding in their manipulation of the stock price.

You're probably already wondering, so I'll answer the question that I'm sure is on your mind. In those early dealings with Stratton, I wasn't innocent or taken advantage of. I wanted in, and I got there in my usual way, by launching a full-on charm school offensive. If Jordan was a shark or a wolf, then I was like a mini-barracuda in my own right.

In our first conversation, Jordan mentioned that he liked to play golf, so we started playing together regularly, along with Danny, Dean, and Jordan's friend Bryan Herman, who owned a similar brokerage firm called Monroe Parker in Westchester. It felt good to be back on the course for the first time in more than a decade.

Getting back into golf also gave me an opportunity to reconnect with my brother John, who now had two young boys and had taken golf up too. We often met up for a game when I was traveling for business. But more important, golf was part of the way I intentionally went about becoming friends with Jordan and the other guys from Stratton. I knew they were working me, and I was working them too. They were wild and using like crazy, while I went to meetings every day and worked hard to stay clean. My mind was clear, or at least as clear as it could be, while theirs were often muddled. I knew this gave me an advantage in some important ways.

At the same time, I was naïve when it came to the deals themselves. When I first became involved with Stratton, I didn't know that what they were doing was illegal. Bear Stearns cleared all of Stratton's trades, so there was a veil of propriety over everything they did. I did not believe that Bear Stearns would be involved with something blatantly illegal, so I just assumed that what they were doing was allowed, or that at the very least it was a grey area.

The first deal they brought me in on as a flipper was for Ropak Laboratories. Ropak Labs sold kits to test the safety of certain drugs and chemicals. At least that's how I understood it. It really didn't matter what they did. I bought the stock at four dollars a share before the IPO, and then the boys at Stratton did their thing. By getting on the phone and hyping up their clients using Jordan's beautifully crafted scripts, they got the price of the stock up to twelve dollars a share. Once the stock price hit its peak, I sold off all my shares.

That first time, I made twenty-five grand in one day. That was more money than I had ever had at one time in my life, and I put it right back into my business. This allowed me to breathe for a second about our cash flow, and it gave me the capital I needed so badly to grow. Before the day was over, I was already hungry for the next deal.

I didn't touch one pill while I was in the heat of my relationship with Stratton Oakmont, but make no mistake. I was no less of an addict than when I was eating pills by the fistful. Money was my new drug, and in the hands of an addict it is just as toxic a substance. By the time I realized that what we were doing was illegal, I was fully on board the merry-go-round, and I couldn't get off, even if I had wanted to.

I could say I wish I hadn't done it, but that's an empty thing to say. More than that, I wish I hadn't been compelled to do it. I wish I didn't have the feeling back then that money was everything. I can tell you now that it's not everything. Not even close. But that was my core belief back then, and once I was hooked, I would have done anything.

04
COLLAR

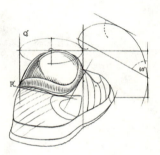

collar • the top edge of the quarter, where you insert your foot.
it is often padded for extra comfort.

For months, Nick and Sal had been late with my commission payments, and it was starting to become a big problem. The eleven hundred dollars I'd used as startup capital was long gone, and I had put the money I'd earned flipping stocks for Stratton back into the company to ramp up production. Without those commissions coming in on time, I had no way to stay afloat.

But I wasn't going to let this sink me. I'd been in the business long enough to know people at plenty of other factories and could make my shoes elsewhere. I knew this might piss off Nick and Sal, but if they weren't going to pay me on time, I wasn't going to worry too much about how they felt.

After I started producing my shoes at a few different factories, Nick and Sal got the message pretty quickly and just fell off. I don't remember even having a conversation with them about it, although I'm sure I did. The important thing was that our business arrangement was terminated, and I was free to go on my way.

It was the spring of 1990, and I started producing the majority of my shoes at a little factory in Queens, which has now been the Steve Madden headquarters for thirty years. Today it's a massive office space that houses hundreds of our employees, a shipping facility, and another building across the street that is the home base for our marketing and finance divisions. At the time, it was just a cramped industrial space with a desk inside that served as a makeshift office. It sat inside a Tudor-style building that looked as though it had been coughed up out of a fairy tale and landed in the middle of a manufacturing zone in Queens. It was only marginally nicer than Sal's beat-up factory out in Brooklyn.

I took over the business side of Steve Madden from Nick and Sal and started working with the Long Island City factory owner, Benny, to make my shoes. The designs, the brand, and the business came together and were finally all mine. So was the responsibility of making it all work, which required bringing on new people.

Miranda had already left to launch her own company, so I needed a new designer to collaborate with me on the shoes. I hired a designer named Linda and made a few more hires as soon as we moved out to Queens. The first was a young woman named Hope I knew from the Five Towns, who became my assistant. She was sweet and meant well, but I was new to the whole concept of having employees report to me and delegating tasks to them. Hope was left to her own devices most of the time with little to no direction from me. She often found herself with nothing to do, and I'm sure this was mostly my fault.

It didn't help that I was rarely in the office because I was either at a meeting or driving around with David selling shoes out of the trunk of the Nissan Sentra. One afternoon that first summer, we returned to the office after a long day of sweltering in the Sentra, and I found Hope lounging in the driveway that led into the factory with a reflector out, getting some sun.

I got out of the Sentra shaking my head and peeled a few bills off the roll of cash in my front left pocket. "This doesn't feel like a winning situation for either of us," I said, handing her the money. I didn't blame

Hope, but I knew I would never be the kind of boss who told my employees exactly what to do and how to do it. I needed people around me who were as motivated and driven as I was, who used all of their energy to find the things that needed doing and then went ahead and did them.

This meant I needed a new assistant, and I mentioned it one day while I was out playing golf with the guys from Stratton. "This girl Wendy I'm dating would be perfect," said Greg, who worked in corporate finance at the firm, as we waited for Dean to take his swing. "She actually used to work for a little shoe company called L. J. Simone." The shoe business, like most industries, is a small world, and I loved the idea of hiring a former L. J. Simone employee.

Wendy Ballew came in to meet with me that week. She was only nineteen years old and had moved to the city from Oregon. In many ways, she still seemed like a country girl, but she was determined to reinvent herself and create a life in the city. She was stylish and had beautiful green eyes and big features that made her look exotic, but I was more impressed by her quiet, calm countenance that I knew would be a good match for my skittish energy. I liked her right away, although it didn't even cross my mind that Wendy and I might ever share anything but a professional relationship.

Finding Wendy was serendipitous. For years, whenever I was in the office, we sat across from each other at the same desk as she went from assistant to customer service representative, office manager, secretary, and receptionist all in one. Eventually she became our director of operations. I watched in awe as she worked. I was a hustler who made good shoes, but I was often gruff with the customers and constantly landed in trouble. Wendy smoothed everything over, kept me in line, organized the complicated shipping and receiving processes, and charmed every single customer with her steady, reliable presence. At the same time, she was a self-starter who intuited what needed to be done and was always looking for new ways to improve how the company was run.

The guys at Stratton were still waiting for the right time for them to take Steve Madden public. In the meantime, they recommended that I hire someone to manage our finances and introduced me to a guy named Arvind Dharia. Arvind and I didn't have much in common, but that was the whole point. He was a whiz with the numbers who came in and organized and legitimized our business dealings, transforming us from a scrappy startup to a still scrappy but far more professional outfit. I was thankful that Arvind expertly handled all the bills and invoices.

These early hires were critical to my success. For a long time, the entire company was just Wendy, Linda, Arvind, David, and me. We were an odd group, but somehow, we just meshed. Steve Madden would not be the company it is today, or have become much of a company at all, really, without each of them.

David went from being my doorman to my driver to being in charge of shipping and receiving to managing multiple warehouses for us. Meanwhile, Arvind took us from a company that subsisted off of rolls of cash to a large-scale corporation, although in my mind and at our core we're still the same inelegant and hard-driving startup. He has been the CFO of Steve Madden since 1992, when that really didn't mean much of anything, until today when it means quite a lot. And Wendy . . . well, we'll get to that a little later.

Linda, on the other hand, didn't stay with the company long, but she helped design some of our most iconic early shoes. After I split from Nick and Sal, the first shoe we designed, built, and invoiced under the name Steve Madden was the Marilyn. At first, I just wanted to make a clog. I had been making clogs of various styles since back at L. J. Simone and sold them even earlier at both Toulouse and Jildor. I had worn clogs back in college and always had an affinity for them. I still love making clogs today. The magic of clogs is that they're versatile. Women can wear clogs with dresses, skirts, or pants. You can put them on high heels, flats, or a platform and use all kinds of colors and materials. This time, though, I wanted to do something different.

At our little desk in the factory, Linda sketched while I tweaked the design to make it less traditional and more feminine. As we worked, the heel grew narrower and eventually went from a typical block style to a higher cone-shape. The toe became pointier, giving it a streamlined, minimalist look. What had started off as a clog became more of a mule. Those two words are often used interchangeably, but a mule tends to have a higher heel and lack the platform that's more typical of a clog.

After a while, I turned to Linda. "That's it. Look at that," I said, snatching the paper she was sketching on right out of her hands. "From the front it will look like she's wearing boots, but it's open in the back," I said, pointing at it with my finger. "That's a great shoe," I said emphatically. "This is going to be a hit."

What can I say? I was right. I named that shoe the Marilyn after Marilyn Monroe, even though it wasn't remotely the kind of shoe she would have worn. I just thought it was a sexy shoe, and it deserved to be named after the ultimate fantasy girl.

We made the first Marilyn right there in that little factory in Queens. First, David and I drove to the Garment District to get the leather and other materials. Then we went back to the factory and gave it all to the sample maker along with the sketch Linda had drawn. They produced samples, always in a size six, which I loaded into my sample bags and took with me to the stores. When a store ordered shoes, we wrote all our invoices out by hand in that tiny shared office inside the factory.

For the next several months, a sample of the Marilyn sat in the place of honor on the dashboard of the Nissan Sentra as David and I drove from one end of the city to the other selling it into stores. When I was in a good mood, I put my feet up on the dashboard and held the shoe in my lap, feeling and smelling the leather as I sang along to the country music on the radio. I was so excited about the Marilyn that the buyers at all the stores couldn't help but get excited too. And from day one, the buyers at every store we went to wanted the Marilyn.

Early on, part of my luck was that I had so little competition within the shoe business from my peers. It seemed like all the sharp, young people my age were working on Wall Street, so my competition was pretty much all coming from companies that had been in business for decades and still did things the same old ways. It was an older industry creating products for an older clientele. This enabled me to step in and be disruptive, though that term didn't exist back then. I wasn't a kid. I was in my thirties, but as far as the shoe business was concerned, I might as well have been wearing a diaper.

Fashion was not only geared toward older folks, but it also focused completely on the elite. There were luxury, high-end brands and lower-priced, discount brands. The two were totally separate, and it seemed like there was nothing in between. My shoes filled that space and appealed to the Generation X girls who couldn't afford or didn't want to wear the styles they saw in fashion magazines.

Soon enough, the same types of Gen X girls that I used to stop on the street to ask about their shoes were actually wearing the Marilyn. That's when I knew we had some magic and could really build a business, but I still had no idea how far it would go.

The shoes I'd designed in the past had sold well, but the Marilyn was my first unadulterated hit. Seeing a girl on the street wearing the Marilyn was how I imagined it would feel to hear your own song on the radio. In many ways, a great shoe is a lot like a hit song. It sparks a similar kind of gut-level response using roughly the same combination of art and commerce to create something that people want to have in their lives.

That year, 1991, I took out a big booth at the annual shoe show in New York City. Inspired by L. J. Simone, I played music and created a rock-and-roll vibe, trying to come off as a bigger player in the shoe world than I really was. Meanwhile, I paced back and forth in our booth like a caged animal with a shoe in my hand, racing around to make sure every buyer saw whatever sample I was most excited about at that moment. And it worked. People flocked to the booth, lining up to look at our shoes and write orders right then and there. It was incredible.

Despite this success and the influx of money from my dalliances with Stratton, I still constantly struggled with cash flow. This is something that most people who haven't started a business themselves don't understand. They see people wearing your shoes or buying your products and assume this means you have plenty of cash in the bank. But this is far from the truth. So, let's break it down really quick.

By this point, I had taken the factory over from Benny, so it was all on me. No one else was footing the bill for the materials, the employees, the rent on the factory, nothing. Say, for instance, we received a huge order from a department store for a thousand pairs of the Marilyn. That was great, but we wouldn't get paid until after those shoes were shipped and received. This meant we had to have cash in the bank to fund the entire production of those shoes without relying on stores to pay their invoices.

But it got worse. Then there was the fact that many retailers were late with their payments. So, how was I supposed to make more shoes for the next order and pay my staff? Finally, when a store bought too many pairs of a shoe and they didn't sell, they could return them and get their money back. But where was that money supposed to come from? Oh, yeah, and I hadn't paid my rent or eaten yet in this equation, either.

It all added up to the fact that we were stretched uncomfortably thin even though we were doing so well. This, of course, led me back to Stratton. Those guys had the exact opposite of a cash flow issue. They had *too* much cash floating around and eventually went to some pretty great lengths to hide some of it. They spent the rest like there was no tomorrow on yachts, cars, multiple homes, and watches that cost tens of thousands of dollars apiece.

To motivate the brokers at Stratton, Danny would tear up one-hundred-dollar bills and scream that if a few measly hundreds were worth anything to them, they should go and work at McDonald's. Those guys were out of their minds, but it also seemed as if they had planted a money tree in the middle of Stratton's offices. That was impossible to resist, at least for me.

One night, Jordan called me up and asked, "What are you doing to-night?" I told him I was working, but he insisted, "Meet me by the river on Thirty-Fourth Street." When I got there, a helicopter was waiting to take us to Atlantic City, where we ate steaks and lobsters and Jordan bet and lost at least half a million dollars without batting an eye. Meanwhile, I was scraping together every nickel I could find just to stay in business. So, when they asked, I was happy to flip stocks by buying and selling shares on the day of a company's IPO and make a quick twenty to forty grand that I could invest in the business.

Today, I liken those deals to taking a shortcut. They helped me solve my cash flow issues at the time, but, like most shortcuts, they weren't actually the best way to get to my destination. If I could go back and tell myself one thing, I would say to be more patient. I have no doubt that with the right team and the right products, we could have made it without taking a shortcut. But I'll never know for sure.

At least I wasn't frivolous with the money. Every penny I made, I immediately put back into growing the business, making more shoes, and hiring more people. I was incredibly lucky to find people who were as obsessed as I was, who understood what I was trying to do and didn't mind that I expected them to work 24/7 like I did.

When I wasn't at the factory, I was either at a meeting or sitting in a department store studying women shopping for and buying shoes. I was fully engaged, all the way on, and always working. I loved it, building and struggling and clawing my way forward. And I have no doubt that devoting myself so fully to the business helped me stay clean. I had a purpose, a passion, and, sure, you could say that work, like money, was a powerful drug.

One morning, a guy showed up to my meeting who wasn't a regular at that particular location, though he had been sober for quite a while. When it was his turn to share, he talked about how he had worked in the shoe industry back in the 1970s and was eventually driven out of business because of his addiction. He told us stories of traveling to Europe and Asia to sell shoes and hiding drugs in his sample cases. I knew I had found a kindred spirit.

After the meeting, I walked up and introduced myself. "I'm Peter," he said, shaking my hand. I told him that I was in the shoe business and invited him to join me and Eddie and some of the other guys at Lanciani for coffee. Peter Migliorini became a part of this crew, and we began to spend a lot of time together. After a while, I asked him to be my sponsor.

On the weekends, Peter would meet me at shoe stores all over the city, and we would sit there and talk as I analyzed what made women buy certain shoes. This told me more about how trends were evolving than any fashion expert could have. Today, trend forecasting is an entire industry, but this old-fashioned method always worked for me.

More than anything, I loved to watch a woman try on a pair of my shoes. Seeing the shoes in the context of her outfit, how she walked in them, and the way she beveled in front of the mirror gave me a completely different perspective that I found inspiring. It was almost magical how the shoes came to life before my eyes when they went from the shelf to the foot. On the shelf, they just sat there, inanimate. And then, once a woman put them on, suddenly they were alive, like the toys in the movie *Toy Story*, breathing and talking and revealing their secret world.

Working constantly and obsessively left little time for my relationship with Paula. We had been dating for a couple years when I asked her to marry me. Our relationship wasn't perfect at that point and hadn't been for a while. I wanted to make it work, but I simply didn't know how.

I loved her and figured the next step would be to get married. Maybe that would help fix things.

It's hard to say exactly what has caused the problems in my relationships, but it's something I've struggled with my entire life. Surely the ADHD doesn't help. But blaming it completely on that almost feels too neat, like an easy out. The truth is that relationships are the one area of my life that I've never been able to successfully cobble together.

Part of me believes that I deserve a break for this. I've tried to do good in my life, and in most areas I would say that I've succeeded. But whatever it is within me that led me to create all this can't be turned off. It's part of the package. I'm excessive. Excessively aggressive and excessively selfish with an excessive work ethic and excessive drive. It's all one. I'm not making excuses for my bad behavior. I admit that I've done some shitty things. But at the end of the day, you have to look at the balance sheet.

I loved being with Paula, but I was rarely present with her. Those four screens in my brain kept me too stimulated and otherwise engaged, thinking about our current line of shoes, our next Steve Madden shoe show, the upcoming deal I was doing with Stratton, and, wait a minute, what are those shoes that woman is wearing? After we got engaged, Paula and I continued to drift apart. Our relationship ended before Steve Madden really had a chance to take off.

I didn't stop to mourn the relationship. I was too driven to keep pushing forward at all costs. Next on the horizon was opening a Steve Madden store. This had been on my mind for a long time, even though almost no shoe designers at the time had their own retail locations. I had seen at both Toulouse and Jildor how important a woman's experience at the store level was. What went on at the store ultimately determined which shoes she was going to buy. The only way to control this experience and encourage her to buy my shoes instead of a competitor's was to have my own Steve Madden store. It would also be a great way to get the entire collection directly in front of consumers without having to go through buyers, although we still went through buyers to get our shoes into other stores too.

I wanted our first store to be unique and interactive, not just a typical shoe store that you could find anywhere. The first unexpected thing we did was to choose a location in SoHo. This area, south of the Village where I lived, had housed artists' studios and warehouses for decades. There were almost no residential properties in the neighborhood and very few retail locations. But over time, tourists had gravitated to SoHo to visit the artists, and art galleries began popping up along with a few restaurants and boutiques to cater to these tourists. It was still a risky location for a relatively unknown brand, but I knew it would give us some street cred to be located in this edgy, hipster part of town.

When it came to setting up the store itself, I wanted to create a real experience for customers. Now many retail stores are interactive and experiential, but this was unheard of at the time. We blasted cool music and featured a large serenity garden right by the front door. That store was like my first baby. Before we opened our doors, I obsessed over every little detail, from the shoe displays to the staff we hired to work the floor.

The day we opened in May of 1993, I was terrified that we wouldn't sell one shoe. And business was slow at first. SoHo has since become the biggest shopping destination in New York City, but there wasn't much foot traffic in the area back then. Finally, a woman came in and bought a pair of brown suede boots with a big buckle around the ankle. I hadn't experienced the same mixture of excitement and relief since I lost my virginity.

We kept the factory in Queens and moved our office, if you could even call it that, to the back of the store in SoHo. It was really just one desk that Wendy and I shared. The two of us and the salesclerks at the store started spending so much time together that we developed a familial relationship. We worked hard, but we also found time to joke around and laugh together. I loved being in the store and even working the floor. I'd see a woman come in and guess what shoes she'd like just by getting a quick sense of her overall aesthetic. After a long day of driving around with David selling shoes, I would ask him to drop me off at the store so I could put in a few more hours either selling on the floor or in the back with Wendy sorting through invoices and shipping out shoes.

Meeting our customers directly at the store gave me great insight into the type of young women who were actually buying our shoes. I wanted to know everything about them: what movies they liked, what music they listened to, where they bought their clothes, and, most important, what they wanted in a shoe. Styles were changing fast, and I had to keep up.

As the 1990s took hold, music and fashion were coming together in a new way, and now it was all about grunge. Those teen grunge girls were rebellious and cool, and their look was reminiscent of the 1970s, with tight knit tops and bellbottoms. This was an era I was familiar with, and I created shoes to fit in with the trends of the time that had a more aggressive, almost masculine look with a rock star edge.

The first one of these shoes to really take off was the famous Mary Lou, a new take on the Mary Jane with a big round bump toe, a platform heel, and a sexy, baby doll vibe. Baby doll dresses had infiltrated the grunge fashion scene, and the beauty of the Mary Lou was that it looked great with the white frilly lace dresses teenage girls were wearing to clubs *and* the ripped jeans and fishnets that epitomized grunge.

It was this shoe that I brought with me to Stratton Oakmont on the day of Steve Madden's initial public offering in the fall of 1993, just six months after our first store opened in SoHo. Danny had asked me to come in and give a speech that morning for the Stratton brokers. Jordan himself was famous for getting up in front of that rabid group, microphone in hand, and hyping them up to sell the crap out of whatever shitty company they were taking public that day. He was the most charismatic public speaker I had ever seen, and he knew exactly what to say and how to say it to get those guys, and the few women on their team, pumped.

To put it mildly, I was not nearly as polished or convincing. Sure, I knew how to turn on the charm and be charismatic when working with an individual buyer or a customer or even Jordan himself. But I wasn't exactly in the habit of performing in front of a crowd, never mind a crowd like this. Danny had told me to be there, though. He said it would get the guys excited to meet me and explained that this would help them sell the stock, which meant more money for the company.

So, there I was with the microphone in one hand and the Mary Lou in the other. As I'd predicted when we first came up with the design, the Mary Lou was taking off across the country. It was the first Steve Madden shoe that really defined our customer base. The girls wearing our shoes had always trended younger, but plenty of women in their thirties and up had also worn the Marilyn and our other styles. The Mary Lou, though, was almost exclusively embraced by the Gen X teens, and this is when we began doggedly pursuing that market. I related to those punk rock girls wearing our shoes who felt like outsiders. I may not have dressed like them, but they were still very much my people, and I was grateful to have them as my core customers.

I naïvely thought the Stratton brokers would be interested in hearing about this. "This shoe right here is the Mary Lou," I said into the mic, trying to be heard over the din of the large crowd that had no interest whatsoever in what I was saying. "It's really a take on the Mary Jane." The guys were shouting to one another from across the room, laughing, and basically ignoring me, but I pressed on, holding out a sample of the Mary Lou. "See that big bump toe? That's what makes it really unique."

Out of nowhere, I felt something hit me in the right shoulder. A shoe. Then I felt another hit my stomach and one at my chest. Instinctively, I ducked before I could even process the fact that these guys were throwing my own shoes at me. I'd brought in several pairs for them to pass around and take home to their wives or girlfriends. But they truly did not care what I was saying or what I stood for or even what kind of shoes I made. I was just a name on a piece of paper that they could sell.

Luckily, Jordan saved me by grabbing the microphone and giving his own much more inspiring speech, and I got out of there as quickly as possible. It was a weird experience, but it didn't really bother me. I would have stood there while they threw shoes at me all day if it meant making more money for the company.

As Jordan had promised, before the IPO I had already received roughly half a million dollars as an early investment from a few of the guys at Stratton. I had quickly used that money to ramp up production. Those early investors received shares of Steve Madden stock on the day of the IPO in exchange for those funds. That day, the three million available shares of authorized Steve Madden stock were valued at fifteen million dollars, a truly ludicrous amount for a company with one store and a few pairs of hot shoes. But there you had it.

Stratton could have taken as big a bite out of these shares as they wanted. They called the shots, and they went for a huge gulp. Jordan decided that they would keep 85 percent of those shares. They ended up selling about half of them, or roughly 40 percent of the company, to the public on the day of the IPO, and Stratton kept the rest. The remaining 15 percent went to me.

This was an unfair deal, and I knew it. A founder should retain far more than 15 percent of his or her own company at the IPO—30 percent would have been more appropriate. But I also knew that no other firm was going to give me the money I needed to grow, so I was willing to take what I could get. And even then, I had a bit of a revenge scheme in mind. Or call it a rebalancing effort.

See, technically it was illegal for Jordan to hold so many shares as the underwriter of the public offering. So, he asked me to hold one point three million shares of the company in my name, even though they really belonged to him. Those shares were worth four million dollars at the time and would have a value of somewhere around ninety million dollars today. They were like an insurance policy for me, my way of ensuring that Jordan didn't steal my own company right out from under me. Although I had agreed to hold them for Jordan, I had no intention of ever returning them.

Within an hour of the market opening, the Stratton brokers drove the price from four dollars and fifty cents a share up to eighteen dollars a share through cold calls and intimidation. Yes, their tactics ruined the finances of many people who invested in some of Stratton's other companies. But Steve Madden was different. No one expected us to become a real company worth investing in—not Jordan, not the brokers at Stratton, and in my weakest moments, not even me. But if you had bought Steve Madden stock that day, even at the inflated price, and held onto it, you would be very rich today.

As for me, I went from constantly worrying about cash flow to being a multi-millionaire within three hours. It was a lot like winning the lottery. But as most people who have actually won the lottery will tell you, the fantasy and the reality are not the same. I knew Stratton had manipulated the stock and that the whole thing was probably too good to be true, but I told myself it was another grey area. Maybe it wasn't exactly ethical, but it wasn't strictly illegal, either.

Deep down, a part of me knew this was bullshit, but the thought allowed me to sleep at night and use that money to rapidly grow the company and hit the next level of success. This in turn earned money for those unwitting investors and put food on the table for our rapidly growing number of employees and their families. How could that be immoral?

That money and the opportunities it provided came easier than they should have. I freely admit that. But in the end, it was all very expensive. I paid for it, and then some.

05
VAMP

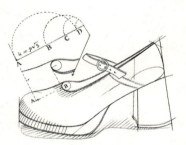

vamp • the section of upper that covers the front of
the foot as far back as the join of the quarter.

"Steve, you've got to check out this book." I was pacing around the Steve Madden booth at the shoe show when a customer named Joe Carvelli approached me. Joe was a buyer for two shoe stores out in the Hamptons, and he was holding out a book. I set down the shoe samples I was holding and glanced at the title: *Driven to Distraction*.

"Very funny," I told Joe, looking around to see how buyers were responding to our newest line. The booth was packed, which was always a good sign.

"No, I mean it, Steve," he said, forcing the book at me. "You could've written this book . . . or it could've been written about you. Check it out, I'm telling you."

"Alright, alright!" I tucked the book under my arm just to appease him. But part of me was intrigued. *Driven to Distraction* was the first popular book about ADHD. Before then, it was something only a few psychologists took seriously and that most people thought was either made up or only affected a few kids. *Driven to Distraction* shed new light on ADHD as a very real condition that affects many kids and adults too.

I spent that entire night tearing through the book, feeling like I was seeing myself fully for the first time. It was painful and reassuring at once to read the list of symptoms that I'd been blaming myself for my entire life: the sloppiness, the inability to keep track of important items, the temper tantrums, the negative impact that all of this has on relationships . . . check, check, check, check.

Of course, not everyone with ADHD is the same, but that book confirmed that I had a classic, undeniable case. The question wasn't whether or not I had it but what, if anything, I was going to do about it.

I had started going to therapy at around the time I'd gotten sober, and I asked my therapist, who I still see today, what she thought about the possibility of me being diagnosed with ADHD. She agreed that I exhibited pretty much all the symptoms and arranged for me to get officially tested and diagnosed. But right before the appointment, I cancelled. It was clear to me that I had this thing, but I also knew that I wasn't going to take medication if they ended up recommending it. So, what was the point of going through all that?

Let's be clear about something: The meds for ADHD are amphetamines, which are addictive, mood altering, stimulating drugs. Now, I understand that for people with ADHD, amphetamines improve brain function in the cortex—for me it's more like a vortex—so you can focus. It's entirely possible that they would have helped me, especially when I was younger. In my efforts to self-medicate I had almost killed myself with drugs and alcohol. But now that I was clean, I didn't want to take any drugs that might jeopardize my sobriety. Plus, I was keenly aware that ADHD, now that I had a name for it, had helped me just as much as it had hurt me.

Yes, it hurt me, primarily when it came to relationships, but in other ways too. Most of the time, I had trouble following conversations. I lost my concentration easily, missed appointments, and was always terrible at follow-up. Those were clearly all symptoms of ADHD. But on the flip side, I had the ability to hold half a dozen thoughts in my head at once, to follow the plotlines on all four of those screens in my mind. If I cut this down to one screen, maybe I would have been calmer and more focused, but I feared that I'd also be less effective.

Ideas were like fireworks going off in my mind every two seconds, a constant wave of thoughts about who I was going to hire next, how to boost sales, the designs for next year's line, and on and on. Sure, this influx was frustrating and even debilitating at times. There were moments when I lamented why I had to be this way. But at other times, I saw how it was helping me do so many different things at once.

The market moves fast, and my constant shifting from one idea to the next helped me keep up. It often frustrated my team. As soon as we agreed to focus on wedges, I'd derail the conversation by bringing them a cowboy boot. But this helped us stay ahead of trends and keep up with fickle consumers. We became known for our speed to market, and to a great extent this was thanks to the intense speed of my thoughts and ideas.

To compensate for the downsides of my ADHD, I had found people who were amazing at handling the things that completely sidelined me. Most successful entrepreneurs will tell you to hire around your weaknesses, and I'd been doing this for years without even realizing it. I'd also created little workarounds so I could do my own job as effectively as possible.

I saw now that my cash payroll way back before Arvind properly organized the company was actually a coping mechanism for ADHD. That's why I could never pay my bills. And my terrible driving record was in part due to distraction, even when I was sober. Hiring people like David to handle the driving, Arvind to manage our finances, and Wendy to organize the rest of the company took the pressure off of me and allowed me to focus exclusively on the ideas exploding in my mind.

Now that we had the capital we needed, I prioritized hiring more talented people so I was free to obsess over our products. One of these people was Rachelle Watts, a shoe designer who quickly became my chief collaborator and is still with the company. I first met Rachelle when she came to our booth at the shoe show. At the time, she worked for a company that accumulated information about hot shoes and then took that intel to Payless or J. C. Penney to sell them to a bigger market—a shoe spy.

I didn't suspect anything because Rachelle fit right in with the other young women who worked for me with her downtown, rock-and-roll clothes and brassy dyed-red hair. She joined us for a cigarette right in the middle of our suite in the Plaza. "I love your energy," she told me. "Your shoes are so cutting edge, and they're my personal taste. I'd give anything to work for you."

I hired Rachelle, and we quickly got in synch and began designing some great shoes together. We would sketch out an idea in the office, make the shoe right there in the Long Island City factory, and then place it in the SoHo store almost immediately. This allowed us to market-test our designs and see how the buyers reacted to the shoes before launching a larger-scale production.

Other times, I'd call Rachelle from the SoHo store and describe an idea I had for a shoe—something I had dreamed up or a twist on a style I had seen a young woman wear into the store. Then Rachelle sketched it out based on my description, had a sample made in the factory, and brought it to me at the store. I'd either love it or hate it. Over time, she got better at interpreting my harried descriptions, and the shoes she brought to the store more closely matched my initial vision. Our speed to the market became even more important later as the business grew, and it gave us an edge even in those early days of 1994.

Despite the benefits of having our own factory, I knew we could expand more quickly if we started importing shoes. I hired a consultant to help me find the right person to make this happen. "I need someone who really understands the import business," I told him over steak frites at Barolo, an Italian restaurant on West Broadway right near the store. "Someone like John Basile." John was a few years older than me and had been working at L. J. Simone for the past few years, rapidly expanding their import business after I'd left.

The consultant, Steve Drescher, earned his entire fee with his next sentence: "Then why not hire John Basile?" It had never occurred to me that I could do that! As much of a hustler as I was, I was still stuck thinking small in so many ways. The fear of poverty that I'd grown up with lived deep in my bones, and I often caught myself running around like Chicken Little, thinking the sky was about to fall.

My constant worry kept me on my toes and prevented me from making careless moves with the company. I was cautious, and that was a good thing, but it would have held us back if I didn't have people around me to help me think bigger.

Hiring John Basile to run our wholesale business was one of the best decisions I ever made. We quickly rose to a new level as a company, and he was the main force behind this progress. But we argued constantly. I was a hard driver, but I still wanted to take conservative bets instead of placing large orders. John was the opposite. He was the kind of guy who could make a company huge or put it out of business in a single day. We were like the turtle and the hare, going to the mat almost on a daily basis about whether slow and steady or fast and furious would end up winning the race.

I admit that my conservative approach sometimes made it more difficult for us to be taken seriously. John traveled to Brazil and Mexico to find factories and set up accounts with them. Rachelle and I continued to design shoes in Long Island City, and then we sent our designs to those factories and imported the shoes they made. But when we went through the whole process of making a deal with a new factory and then placed an order for something like only sixty pairs of shoes, they were pissed off. And rightfully so. We did our best to sell them on the dream that eventually we would become the preeminent shoe designer for young people in the United States. But until that happened, we often had to jump from factory to factory when they got sick of our small runs.

It was worth it, though, to have our shoes made overseas, because their factories produced shoes in much higher quantities than we could make ourselves. This meant losing the bespoke nature of the shoes, which I found difficult at first. The shoes we made domestically had a rough, handmade feel that I thought was cool. When we got our first shoes in from overseas, they felt too perfect and uniform to me. But I knew that if we wanted to grow, we had no choice but to produce our shoes in bulk. I embraced it, and once I got used to the mass-produced shoes, I realized that this was how they were always meant to look.

Plus, producing shoes overseas made the entire transaction so much cleaner. Instead of worrying about paying for individual materials and labor and insurance, we just bought shoes and sold shoes. Simple.

But John and I were butting heads too often. My solution was to hire a young guy named Mark Jankowski who worked for one of our biggest clients in St. Louis, a company called Edison Brothers that no longer exists. Mark was a kindred spirit, one of the few guys my age I had met in the shoe business who could match my intense energy level. I knew he'd be a good fit for the company.

The problem was that I had to find a way to poach Mark from his employer without pissing them off and losing their business. Somehow, I convinced Mark to quit his job, assuring him that, after a few months, I would call his former employer and explain that he hadn't been able to find a new job and that I wanted to help him out by offering him a position. I had every intention of following through, but I was actually surprised when Mark agreed to this plan.

Mark went ahead and quit. Soon after, before I officially hired him, he came with John and me on a scouting trip to Italy. We often went to Europe and South America, and my eyes were on the ground the entire time, looking at women's shoes. We figured it would be safe for Mark to join us since no one from Edison Brothers would be there, but someone must have seen us together and ratted.

As soon as we got back to the States, I got an angry phone call from the head of Edison Brothers, cancelling all his orders. Edison Brothers was responsible for maybe a third of our profits, and just like that, they were gone. It was a devastating blow for a fledgling company. To this day, I never hesitate to remind Mark of how expensive he was.

Thankfully, another scouting trip soon after helped us recoup those lost profits, and then some. On one trip to northern Italy in 1994, I noticed a lot of women wearing these great leather penny loafers. Though loafers were a classic style that had been around for ages, there weren't a lot of women in the United States wearing them at the time. I saw this as an opportunity.

I brought a few pairs of shoes home from Italy, and Rachelle and I immediately started working on adapting the designs to make them more in line with the quintessential Steve Madden style. We added a stacked heel and a slightly pointed, feminine toe that was reminiscent of the Marilyn. Then we sent the design for those penny loafers to our factory in Brazil, and they turned out beautifully.

Thanks to those shoes, over the next year or two we went from a hot shoe brand to *the* hot shoe brand. Every high school girl across the country *had* to have a pair of those penny loafers. We were still making shoes for rebel outsiders, but now the popular girls were wearing Steve Madden too. For our next line, we tweaked the style to make it even crazier, with a higher platform, a wider heel, and a big bump toe. It was less streamlined and more grunge. Teenage girls loved those shoes because they gave their school uniforms a big edge, and they went on to define 1990s style when they appeared in *Clueless, Friends*, and tons of other films and TV shows.

It was thanks to John that we could keep up with the insane demand for our shoes throughout this period. Despite our disagreements, we were equally obsessed with three things: product, speed, and sales. John was like me to another power. He taught me so much about the industry itself, and I was grateful for the opportunity to jump on his shoulders.

I had learned from my experience at L. J. Simone to bring John in and make him a partner. And I compensated him very well for his work and expertise. Yet, from the beginning, my relationship with John was strained beyond just our fights about the size of our orders. No matter how much autonomy or money I gave him, it was my company. There was no way around this, and as time went on, John grew more and more sensitive to this fact. He did all the work to set up an account with a factory, and then I'd insist on placing a more conservative order than he wanted, and he went crazy. But at the end of the day, it was my call.

I've dealt with this dynamic a lot in my career. My partners are there every day doing the work and putting in the long hours, and they sometimes resent it when it's time to make the final call and it doesn't go their way. I understand this, but at the same time I'm the one taking the risk, so I have to be the one making the calls. There is a plaque on my desk that says, "The Buck Stops Here," and that is simply the God's honest truth.

Every company needs a leader, but this doesn't mean I undermine or micromanage my employees. Letting go has been a thirty-year-plus process. There are just some people who are never going to be comfortable working for a boss. I get it. I was like that too. But I've learned that when this dynamic crops up, it is best for that person to move on instead of sticking around being unhappy working for me.

Years later, I took a page out of the Hollywood book. When they fire a big executive from one of the studios, they often give him or her a production deal to stay on the lot and make their own movies. It's a graceful way to exit and save face. So, I set John up with his own business and bought shoes from him, and we parted ways with no hard feelings.

At the time, though, John's presence allowed me to keep my eye on the big picture and continue growing the company. Mark never really succeeded in his role of mediator, but he did become a critical team member in other ways.

In 1995, as our platform penny loafers were exploding around the country, we opened our second retail store farther uptown in New York City. Next, we wanted to start opening stores in shopping malls. In the New York area, Roosevelt Field, a shopping mall in East Garden City, was the hottest mall at the time, so of course we wanted to start there. The only problem was that they would not return our calls. Our shoes were hot, but our retail business was still too small for a landlord to be willing to take a bet on us. I had to find another way in.

One of our customers was a chain of stores called the Shoe Box that happened to owe us a ton of money for shoes we had sold them. We had been trying to collect on that debt for months. Well, it turned out that the Shoe Box had two stores at Roosevelt Field, so I convinced the owner to give me one of his leases to cancel out the debt.

This was a big win, but the more things started to go our way, the more worried I grew. Things were moving fast, and the last thing I wanted was for our success to be fleeting and unsustainable. That year, I bought myself two pairs of cowboy boots, one black and one green. This sounds like nothing, but it was a huge splurge for me. I never spent money on myself and barely owned any more possessions than I'd had in college. After a few days, I was so wracked with guilt that I had to return one pair of the boots.

I'm still like this. I don't want to buy a new pair of sunglasses for a hundred bucks because I know I'll lose them and it kills me to waste money like that. I don't know if it's due to a lack of self-worth, deeply ingrained cheapness, or both.

I was just as conservative with new hires. My entire family was now living in Florida, and Luke's addiction had really taken hold. We had a warehouse in Florida, so I gave Luke a job there, hoping the stability would be good for him. I didn't know yet that my brother John's drinking was a problem. I saw him much more often than I saw Luke when we met up for a game of golf or when I visited his family in Florida, but he hid it well.

Ever since shutting down Madden Securities, John had been working in the stock market. He seemed to be doing OK, but it wasn't stable. When I saw my parents, which wasn't that often, they seemed worried about him. He had always been the son they were most proud of, but not anymore.

My parents never commented on my success, but they must have known I was doing well. Once in a while, my dad asked me if I could give John a job. "Don't you have anything for him?" he asked, but the idea of hiring someone I didn't really need was outrageous to me, even if it was my big brother.

On the morning we opened in Roosevelt Field, I worked with Mark in the store to make sure everything was ready, down to the last detail. "I'll bet you a hundred bucks we don't do over ten grand today," I told him. Make no mistake—ten grand would be a good day, but I felt the need to make sure our expectations weren't set too high.

"Steve, I've been here for the last couple of weeks setting up," Mark told me. "I see how excited all the girls are. There's no way we do under ten grand." We shook on the bet and finished checking the displays. Soon, it was time to open, and when I went to the front of the store to unlock the door, I saw an amazing sight. Girls were lined up down the mall corridor, past the next three stores at least, just to get in. That day, we did over ten grand in sales before noon.

From that point on, we needed crowd control every weekend at our Roosevelt Field store. It was like the hottest club in the city. I'd work the floor talking to customers, and Mark would act as doorman, letting in a few more girls each time another group left. Of course, the other malls in the area noticed, and they started coming to us offering a lease instead of the other way around. Mark became the default head of retail, opening more and more locations around the country.

Working the floor at Roosevelt Field gave me new insights into our customers. We had intentionally gone after the teen market, but we had also noticed that in the middle of the country women up to the age of fifty or so happily wore our shoes. It was different on the coasts, where we were more firmly established as a teenage brand and had very few customers over thirty. I loved having teens as our core customers, but as the company grew, I wanted our base of buyers to expand too. I believed that older women in New York and Los Angeles would love our shoes if they'd only give them a chance.

Whenever a mother brought her teen girls into the store, I'd show her some shoes I thought would be a good fit for her. "This pair would look great on you," I said, but these women almost always demurred. "No, no, these are for my girls, not for me," they said.

I realized that these women felt self-conscious wearing our shoes because we were so well known as a brand for young girls. I didn't have a solution to this problem yet. Of course, I didn't want to turn off our loyal teen customers by marketing our shoes to their moms, but eventually I wanted to capture their moms as buyers too.

I was still cautious, but I was beginning to see our full potential, and I was obsessed with growing the business and realizing that dream. This meant continuing to play ball with Stratton. Seven million dollars had been enough to get us this far, but to keep expanding a company, there's really no such thing as too much capital. And to an addict, of course, there's never enough. More stores and more employees meant we needed more money.

Plus, by this point, the guys at Stratton were accustomed to me saying yes when they asked me to flip stock for them. I'm no innocent, but Jordan didn't mess around, and it was always clear that if I stopped playing along, it wouldn't have gone over well. And let's be honest—I was hooked. I was working the program and staying sober, but looking back, I can see that I had just switched my addiction from drugs to money. It's so obvious now, but at the time, in the thick of it, I had no idea.

Besides, Jordan and I had become real friends. When he wasn't too whacked out, he was a great coach, always motivating me to push harder and do more with the business. Stratton was still raking in money, but of all the companies they'd taken public, Steve Madden was the only one to really take off. People who had purchased our stock at the IPO could sell it and actually make a profit. This was the antithesis of how most of Stratton's deals went, and I think it gave Jordan a sense of pride. Having Steve Madden in Stratton's portfolio gave them a much-needed shred of legitimacy.

But more than anything, we got along. Jordan would call me up and we'd jump on his private jet to go play golf at some of the best courses around the country. Yes, the plane was often full of high-end prostitutes and enough drugs to kill an entire troupe or two worth of circus animals, but I never partook in any of that. I was getting enough of a high from work and money.

Jordan and I often hung out with Bryan Herman, who was running his own brokerage firm in Westchester, New York, called Monroe Parker, which was like a little brother to Stratton Oakmont. Bryan brought me in on flip deals for his firm, as well, earning me twenty grand or so a pop. I was fully immersed in the pool of sharks, still telling myself that I was a barracuda but really just trying to stay afloat. Jordan, Danny, Bryan, Dean, and I golfed all over the country, flew to Key Largo on weekends, and partied on Jordan's yacht. Well, for them it was a party. For me, it was all work.

I was always thinking about the next deal, the next shoe, the next high, the next sliver of proof of my worthiness and value. When I wasn't golfing with those guys, I spent most weekends visiting our stores to talk to customers and motivate the staff. On a typical weekend, I'd fly to Detroit on Saturday morning, spend the whole day on the floor in one of our stores, fly to Chicago to do the same thing on Sunday, and then fly home that night. Or else I'd just camp myself in the SoHo store or at

Roosevelt Field for the entire weekend. My whole life was the company, and I loved every minute of it.

By then, I had scouts traveling around the world for me looking for promising styles that we could adapt and turn into Steve Madden shoes. I was walking down the hallway of our building in Long Island City on the way to my office when one of these scouts approached me with a shoe he'd found in a factory in Spain. It was a simple slide with a stretchy fabric over the top.

"Wow, this is great," I said, stopping to look more closely at the shoe. I turned it over in my hands, admiring its unique simplicity. Right away, I could see how we would change the style to give it a classic Steve Madden look by putting it on a big platform and widening the toe bed. It would be the perfect summer shoe for all the girls who loved our loafers. "This is going to be huge," I said to the scout before turning around to bring it to Rachelle.

That shoe, the Slinky, became our first million-dollar shoe. That summer, it seemed like every girl in America was wearing the Slinky, shuffling along with her colorful toenails peeking out while the back of the shoe smacked pleasantly against the soles of her feet.

The word *iconic* is thrown around a lot. I've probably used it too many times in this book already. But there is really no other word to describe the impact the Slinky had on the shoe business. If you're a guy or are too young to remember, ask any woman you know who was between the ages of twelve and forty in 1996, and I bet she'll share nostalgic tales of her experiences with the Slinky. Our customers loved it, we were making money, and it felt amazing to be successfully combining art and commerce the way I'd always wanted.

But the high from our success was soon dampened by the fact that there was trouble in the air for Stratton and likely anyone associated with them. I don't know when the feds started talking to Jordan or when he actually began cooperating with them. It had probably been in the works for a while, but to me it seemed sudden when, in 1996, they shut down Stratton Oakmont and barred Jordan and the other principals from the securities trade. All that money and energy and ambition and greed were suddenly gone. *Poof*. It didn't seem real.

No one had been indicted—yet—but it felt inevitable. I tried not to think about it, but the fear that I was going to have to pay for all the deals I'd done with Stratton sat there on my back, weighing me down every day. What was done was done, though. There was nothing I could do at that point but dance in between the rain drops and hope I wouldn't get wet.

In a way, it was ironic that the regulators had shut down Stratton Oakmont, because by then dozens of similar bucket shops had sprung up around them. Stratton had started this trend and had been the most successful, but they were far from the only firm using the same types of schemes. Jordan smartly realized that he could still profit from the industry he had created by betting against the other brokerage companies' worthless stocks. He had a secretary and needed a place to work, so I gave him an office in our building in Long Island City. There, he shorted stocks by borrowing shares and selling them, knowing that since their value was likely inflated at the IPO, he could buy them back later to repay what he'd borrowed at a lower price.

I could tell that some of my staff members felt funny about having Jordan in the office. But what could I do? I had made a deal with the devil, and now the devil was there in the office, swinging a golf club and pontificating on how I should run my business. When Jordan was reasonably sober, we had a great time together. But he was using a lot, and, on most days, he was pretty out of it by noon. I brought him to a few meetings with me and tried to help him get clean, but it didn't stick. I didn't blame Jordan. An impending indictment wouldn't exactly have motivated me to get sober either.

Now that Jordan wasn't making the same kind of money he'd been earning at Stratton, the Steve Madden shares I had allegedly been holding for him since the IPO came back into the picture. Every so often he'd tell me, "Cobbler, I gotta get that stock from you."

I'd just brush it off or tell him, "Let me see what I can do." He'd let it go and bring it up again a few days or weeks later. Like everything having to do with Stratton, I knew it would come back to bite me eventually, but I put it off for as long as possible.

First, bad news came from another direction. During a regular checkup, my father's doctors discovered that he had a tumor. In the middle of the surgery to remove it, my dad had a heart attack. He never made it out of surgery.

He was in his eighties and had been in poor health for a while, but of course my father's death affected me deeply. I spent a lot of time in Florida that winter, helping my mom make arrangements and adjust to life without my dad. By then, I had the money to help her financially, too, and the irony wasn't lost on me that her least favorite son was now the one in a position to help.

Going back and forth between New York and Florida put me off my routine. I wasn't making it to as many meetings as usual, and at night I lay awake thinking about my dad and shoes and Stratton and a million other things. I knew my mom had been having trouble sleeping since my dad's death and was taking sleeping pills, and one night when I couldn't stand it anymore, I went into her bathroom and took some from her medicine cabinet.

If you're not an addict, this probably sounds like no big deal. Who wouldn't need a little help getting to sleep after the death of his father? But to an addict, there is no such thing as a safe dose of a controlled substance. As soon as I had those pills in my body, I had a plan in mind to get my hands on something stronger.

I happened to need to have some dental work done, and as soon as I was back in New York, I went to the dentist. "Can you give me something for the pain?" I asked as soon as the appointment was over. As was my intention, I walked out of his office with my first prescription for Vicodin.

Today, Vicodin almost seems harmless compared to the much stronger opioids that have since flooded the market. It's a combination of opioid and non-opioid painkillers. But it's a highly addictive drug that can be incredibly dangerous and even deadly in the hands of an addict. There is a reason so many people die from opioid addiction. When taken in high doses or combined with alcohol, it can cause you to stop breathing. And high doses are what addicts like me are after. While a regular dose of Vicodin will simply dampen your pain perception, higher doses act on pleasure centers in the brain, creating the feelings of relaxation and euphoria that I was so desperately seeking.

Soon, I was taking seven Vicodin at a time. If I took them too fast, I'd throw up, so I learned to be patient, swallowing each pill one at a time over the course of several minutes. After a few pills, it felt like someone had turned on the burner of a stove at the base of my skull, and a delicious heat rose up in my brain. As soon as it wore off, I needed to find a way to turn that burner back on.

After seven years of hard-won sobriety, I was right back where I'd started, hopeless and helpless in the hands of a substance that was much stronger than I was. My initial prescription was gone in an instant, and then I was on a constant quest for pills.

Addicts are resourceful creatures. Desperation will do that to a person. For a while, I found a pharmacist right near the SoHo store who would sell me Vicodin for one dollar a pill. It was great. I was still working around the clock, and I could just run over any time when I ran out of pills. But then one day he disappeared. I wandered around downtown Manhattan for an entire day searching for him, but he was gone.

I stooped to new lows to score more pills, often calling doctors and begging them to write me a prescription. I always found a way. Whenever I scored pills, my favorite thing to do was to isolate myself in my apartment and get high. Like I said, it was never a party for me. It was more about removing myself temporarily from the world around me. I'd take my pills, peek outside to make sure everything was OK, and then lock the door and enjoy the feeling of warmth rising to my brain.

Of course, my friends from recovery noticed that I wasn't going to meetings and knew exactly what was going on. They tried to get me to go back to meetings, and sometimes I went. I wanted to stop. Of course I wanted to stop. But I just couldn't. Finally, after several months, Peter drove me to an inpatient rehab center in Upstate New York. They gave me methadone so I could detox painlessly and tapered me off slowly so I didn't end up addicted to the methadone.

This did the trick for a time. I was back at work and my daily meetings within a couple weeks. But it was much harder to stay sober now than it had been the first time I'd gotten clean. When I was doing cocaine and quaaludes, I had craved the next high, but with opioids I was literally sick without it. Being hooked on pills felt like being kidnapped. They owned me. Any time I was stressed or not feeling well, my need to find that release would completely take over.

Over the next few years, I slipped many times. Some of these slips lasted months, and others only a day or two. I could blame this on many things. Those next few years would be some of the most stressful of my life. Opioids were and still are far too easy for an addict to get. But at the end of the day, I know that I had no one to blame but myself.

Unfortunately, it was also during these years that my brothers' addictions really pulled them both down. John and Luke spiraled as I spiraled, though I didn't know it at the time.

All told, I detoxed from opioids five times that I can remember, though there may have been even more. Now I worry about the genetic component of this disease every day, but at the time I had what felt like much more urgent things to worry about. Jordan Belfort was after me for his shares, the feds were close behind him for all of my dealings with

Stratton, and I knew there was a long list of other guys in trouble who would gladly rat me out if it meant saving themselves.

If you'd told me then that giving in and paying the price for these crimes would end up being the best possible thing for my sobriety, I would have laughed, or more accurately, cursed you out. Right then, I didn't want to pay. I just wanted to escape. And for as long as I could, that's exactly what I did.

06
WELT

welt • a strip of material that joins the upper to the sole.

Where was she? I had hired Amelia Newton to do customer service, but she was also supposed to be handling inventory. We all had multiple jobs in those days. There was no corporate structure. You were either all in or you were out, and Amelia had seemed all in. She was in her twenties and had left a career in corporate finance to do customer service for us because she loved our shoes. But now we had too much inventory of a platform sandal that was underperforming, and I was mad.

Nothing made me angrier back then than having too much inventory of a shoe because it was such a huge waste of money. I had chased Amelia around our maze-like Long Island City offices, holding up the offending sandal and screaming at her about why she'd ordered so many pairs. When she ran into the bathroom, I pounded on the door with the shoe's impressive heel. "What were you thinking?" But then she snuck right past me and into the office she shared with the entire customer service team, closing the door behind her. Her silence was infuriating, but at least she couldn't hide from me in there.

I stormed into the office just a moment after Amelia had entered, but she was nowhere to be found. There were a few other people in the office, and Mark was sitting on top of Amelia's desk. "Where is she?" I demanded.

I was met with shrugs and blank expressions. Shaking my head, I headed back to my office. She couldn't hide from me forever, and, besides, I had a million other things on my mind. I'd lost my thrill for the chase.

The next morning, we were flying to Maryland for a personal appearance at Montgomery Mall. It was an opportunity to schmooze with buyers and meet with a category of people I'd never had before in my life: fans. This new development was surreal. When I visited malls around the country, young women came up and asked me to sign their shoes or to just give them a hug. This wasn't something I anticipated when I got into the shoe business, but I didn't exactly mind it.

The rest of my team teased me mercilessly. "You're such a rock star, Steve," they said sarcastically. But with everything weighing on me, I figured I might as well enjoy what I assumed would be my fifteen minutes of fame. Besides, I loved meeting the young women who actually wore our shoes. The better I got to know them, the stronger my instincts would be about what they would want to wear next.

As soon as I boarded the plane, I sat down next to Amelia with a big teasing smile. "Where were you yesterday?"

Amelia looked me right in the eye. "I was hiding under my desk," she said coolly, in a New York accent that matched my own. "Mark was covering me by sitting on there so you wouldn't just storm in and fire me for no reason."

I burst out laughing. "Get out of here, really?" I had clearly underestimated her. And, by the way, Amelia (now Amelia Newton Varela) is now the president of Steve Madden.

Without really intending to, I often tested our young hires this way. We had dozens of young women and men in their early twenties who worked at every level in the company. The ones like Amelia who worked hard and were there to learn and grow are now running departments. I demanded a lot from my team and rewarded them mightily when they came through.

The people who couldn't take the long hours or the fast pace left to go elsewhere. Working at Steve Madden wasn't for everyone. It probably wasn't for most people. But the ones who thrived in that environment have done extremely well for themselves and for the company.

Certain things were sacrosanct. If you worked in retail managing a store, you had to be there every Saturday. Saturdays are sacred in retail. If you missed one, there was no place for you in my world. The same thing went for shoe shows and the last day of the quarter, when all managers needed to be in the office to exhort their teams and make sure they made their numbers. We were widely recognized as this cool, hip brand, but at the end of the day, I knew it was hard work, not our talent or even our styles, that would truly set us apart.

When we got to Montgomery Mall, there was a line of girls waiting to meet me, a sight I never really got used to. Right away, I noticed a young woman named Elissa Kravetz who was a student at the University of Maryland. She was wearing a cute pair of our sandals and had a wonderful, positive energy about her. When we held a raffle for a free pair of Steve Madden shoes, I might have told Mark to fix it so she'd win.

A few days later, Elissa sent me a picture of her and six of her sorority sisters all sitting in a circle wearing their Steve Madden shoes with their legs out and their feet touching in the middle. I called her up immediately and asked her to come work for me in marketing. Elissa became something of a muse for me, the epitome of a "Steve Madden girl," who had great instincts and helped me better understand what our customers wanted.

Once again, that season we blew up the shoe show at the Plaza Hotel with an enormous suite, champagne, music, and huge platters of food. It was a big party. My entire team, including Elissa, was running around doing everything possible to make it a huge success. Buyers from all over the country were swarming in to check out our next line of shoes, which included several new versions of the Mary Lou and sandals with huge platforms that were all the rage. I also noticed faces from competing shoe brands circling our suite to see what we were up to.

I always had my show favorites, and that year it was a new take on the Mary Lou on an even higher platform. I had come up with the idea at the last moment after seeing a girl walk into our SoHo store wearing a pair that she had altered herself to add extra height.

When I got into the office later that morning I yelled, "I need Karla!" Karla Frieders worked in our retail department, but, like I said, there was plenty of overlap. "Do we have any sports shoes that are this high?" I asked, spreading my thumb and forefinger several inches apart. Karla shook her head, already knowing what was next. "Do you want me to make a sample?"

"I want it done in time for the show," I said, and, as always, my team made it happen. Now I was carrying that very shoe around, making absolutely sure the buyers from Dillard's, Macy's, and all the other stores saw it.

In the midst of this, I saw another familiar face, but not necessarily a friendly one—Jordan Belfort. He'd moved out of our offices a few months earlier, and I hadn't seen him in a while. I had heard that he was in real trouble and the feds were closing in on him. No one ever really knew what was going on with Jordan. Maybe he was already cooperating with the government. Or maybe he was in denial, hoping to skate just like I was.

As he approached, I noticed that Jordan had dark circles under his eyes. It looked like he either hadn't slept in weeks or was high. I assumed it was both. "Cobbler, I've got to talk to you," he said as he approached.

"What's up, Jordan?" I asked calmly, adjusting the baseball hat I was wearing. For a long time now, I had been losing the long strawberry blond hair that used to be my trademark and had taken to covering it up with a baseball hat. Whenever I was out of the house, I wore one, and as the business had grown more and more successful, other companies noticed and started sending me hats with their logos on them. I never really paid attention to what hat I was wearing at any given moment and inadvertently ended up advertising a lot of random brands on my forehead. Adjusting my hat by wrapping my hands around the brim had become a bit of a nervous habit, something to do with my hands whenever they weren't otherwise occupied.

Jordan and I went down to the lobby to chat. "I want my shares," he told me with intensity in his eyes. "I mean it, Cobbler."

There was something about Jordan's behavior that struck me as odd right away. He seemed nervous, with his eyes darting around the room. I had seen Jordan in many different situations over the years, and *nervous* was never a word I would have used to describe him. I was immediately on guard and began choosing my words carefully. "Alright, let me see what I can do," I said, trying to get rid of him.

"You've been saying that for too long," Jordan said, inching closer to me. "I mean it. You know what I'm talking about, right? The stock that you're holding for me?" I just nodded, which seemed to irritate Jordan further. That's when it occurred to me that he might be wearing a wire. "Think about it, Cobbler, my next step is to take you to court. There's no upside to that. Just give me my shares, and we can both move on with our lives. Trust me, you don't want this hanging over your head forever."

Jordan was convincing, and the whole interaction was just plain weird, but I still didn't take his threat seriously. Maybe it was foolish of me, but I just couldn't imagine that he would want to go to court over this. Our deal for me to hold his shares in a separate corporation under my name wasn't exactly legal. Why would someone who was already on the verge of indictment want to go to court and reveal that?

I knew Jordan had plenty of *chutzpah* and could be vengeful at times, but he wasn't stupid. So, I just kept stringing him along. Besides, I was busy running my company. I didn't have time to worry about giving something back to Jordan that I had never believed was rightfully his.

In the end, I underestimated how vengeful Jordan really was, or maybe just how badly he wanted or needed those shares. Or maybe there was something else going on entirely. Who knows? Jordan was always five steps ahead of everyone else, and it's still not entirely clear what went on between him and the government.

Not long after that shoe show, Jordan indeed filed a lawsuit against me for the one point three million shares. At first, my lawyers and I tried to fight it, intimating in our response that Jordan really didn't want to go to court and open up Stratton's records for scrutiny, but Jordan wouldn't budge.

I was terrified by the prospect of going to court against Jordan. There was a chance the government would use something that was revealed in that lawsuit against me in the future, and there was an even greater chance that I'd lose those shares, which were now worth about twelve million dollars. Meanwhile, Jordan had gone from being one of my closest friends to an adversary seemingly overnight.

Of course, this turn was partly on me. I could have just handed over those shares, but there was no way I was going to do that. The way I saw it, Jordan had been trying to steal my company from me since the day we met. Yes, he had been my only option for getting outside capital back when we were a floundering startup, but he had already profited richly from his early investment—to the tune of more than twenty million dollars. Enough was enough.

In court, Jordan presented the contract we'd signed regarding the one point three million shares. The judge pressed me to admit that the signature on the paper was mine. "It is, Your Honor," I said, hoping I sounded as remorseful as I felt. In that moment, I wished I had never even heard the name *Jordan Belfort*. "But I was manipulated into signing it by someone I trusted as my friend, business associate, underwriter, and confidant."

This was all true. Back when I signed that paper, I had believed it was another grey area. I didn't think Jordan would put himself at risk by signing a contract that was downright illegal. But he had, and without exactly knowing it, so had I.

Jordan and I eventually settled the suit for just over four million dollars. I had to sell off some of my own stock in the company to pay that amount, which really pissed me off. But at the same time, I was glad to be done with the whole thing. The company was doing so well, and those shares were the last remaining string tying Steve Madden, both the company and the man, to Jordan Belfort. I was eager to cut that string and make a clean break. But that did nothing to erase the history between us.

I constantly worried about how I might have to pay for the mistakes of my past. As a distraction, I buried myself in work, looking for new ways to expand. At around this time, I bought a discount shoe store called Shoe Biz in Mineola, Long Island. I did this for two reasons. One, I had gotten to know the store's owner, Rob Schmertz, a young, creative guy who meshed with the rest of the Steve Madden gang. I wanted Rob to be a part of our leadership team. And two, I fancied the idea of expanding Shoe Biz into a line of discount stores. The second part of this plan never came to fruition, but Rob became an instrumental member of our team and stayed on as our brand director for many years.

More than almost anyone else, Rob understood how I wanted the shoes to look, which was incredibly important to me and helped us increase our speed to market even more. Soon, we mastered the art of "test and react." I worked with Rob and the design team on a style, and then we went down to the factory and had a dozen pairs in various sizes cobbled by hand right then and there. Then one of us would jump in a car and bring them down to the SoHo store. There were times when we went from an idea for a style to having the shoes in the store in just three hours.

This gave us a big competitive edge over other popular brands like Nine West and Sam & Libby. There was no such thing as "fast fashion" yet. Most shoe companies designed their entire line of shoes, had them made in a factory somewhere far away, and then sold them to stores maybe six months later. Meanwhile, we were able to anticipate a trend, jump on it, and have a shoe in the store that same day. Then we could immediately see how the customers reacted.

Remember earlier when I said that returns on shoes that didn't sell were a big cash-flow killer? That's why I was so pissed off at Amelia when we had too much inventory of a shoe. Mass-producing a shoe that doesn't hit the mark costs a huge amount of money. Having a sample factory and our own retail stores to test how a style performed helped us avoid that issue almost entirely. When we did a small test run and saw early on that a shoe wasn't working, we could turn it around quickly by tweaking the style, adjusting the price point, or pulling it from the shelves completely.

Though we were all about speed, we were also slavishly devoted to product and never cut corners when it came to making our shoes. At the same time, we knew that our customers were young, so we had to be incredibly sensitive to pricing. Once the teen market embraced our brand, it was extremely important to me to create shoes that our loyal fans could actually afford.

Making shoes is a lot like baking a cake. If you don't use good quality ingredients, the product won't turn out right. So how do you make a cake taste great while using less expensive ingredients, or in our case, how do you craft a shoe that women want to wear for less than a hundred dollars and still turn a profit? This has been one of our main challenges from the very beginning.

It's one thing to create the best shoe possible with no concern about price. You could use the finest materials in the world and make no sacrifices for the highest quality shoes. To me, that's a science. But to make a shoe that a stylish woman can afford and want to wear *and* somehow still make money . . . that's an art. And working within these limitations forced me to be creative.

It took me a long time to embrace the idea of being creative, but it was around this time that I felt I was really in my creative flow—designing products with my team, finding the right people to execute my vision, and putting it all together, much like the movie moguls I'd loved reading about when I was a kid. But at the end of the day, it really all came down to the obsessive work ethic that I learned from my dad and drilled into my team. You could be the most creative, talented person in the world, but without the hustle and grind, you've got nothing.

The jury's still out on whether or not I'm actually talented, but the truth is that talent is not everything. There are plenty of days when I still think I'm not at all talented or creative. But somehow, I've always managed to put things together and create, even if it meant finding people to fill in the gaps for my weaknesses. In a way, that's the most creative endeavor of all.

Believe it or not, one area in which the company was still really sluggish was our advertising. Then, in 1996, I read a cover article in *Vanity Fair* about Kay Thompson, the actress who created the *Eloise* books about a young girl who lived with her nanny in the penthouse of the Plaza Hotel while her rich mother traveled the world. Thompson was Liza Minnelli's godmother, and it's possible that the *Eloise* books were based on her. I found the article and the whole *Eloise* book series fascinating.

What does this have to do with our advertising? Inspiration is funny like that. I can't trace a straight line from *Eloise* to the Steve Madden "big head" ads that we launched in 1997, but I can tell you that *Eloise* was on my mind when I was talking to our marketing team, headed by Tommy Kane at the Hampel/Stephanides advertising agency, about my vision for our ads.

The team came back to me with the idea to use a unique style of photographic manipulation developed by an artist named Butch Belair. Now hybrid animated images like this are commonplace, but when Butch created these distorted images of teenage girls with huge heads and blown-up feet and tiny bodies, shot with a fish-eye lens to warp the image even further, I had never seen anything like it before, and nobody else had either.

Painting those young girls against backdrops around New York City reminded me somehow of *Eloise at the Plaza*. It didn't occur to me at the time that these girls were overly sexualized, though that idea became the subject of controversy and many heated conversations around the office. To me, the bigheaded girls just seemed fashionable and rebellious, a perfect fit for the young women who loved our shoes.

For the first time, I was truly enthusiastic about advertising, and the ads evolved into an exciting collaboration. I worked with Rachelle, Rob, and Elissa to style the models, and became obsessed with choosing the shoes, the clothes, the backdrops, everything. The result was a series of ads that I was incredibly proud of and was happy to spend money on because they were so me, so *us*.

In my heart, the company was still a sort of ragtag outfit, a group of warriors fighting to live another day. Yes, we were focused on profit, but our aesthetic and to some extent our values were different than those of other grown-up, corporate shoe companies. Ever since I was a little boy growing up in the Five Towns, I had always felt like an outsider, and those ads perfectly captured that maverick, defiant sensibility.

See, those ads weren't just successful because they propelled us to another level of awareness and created a brand identity for Steve Madden before people really talked about the idea of having a brand identity. They worked so well because they took the stylish and irreverent identity that we had already internalized, the one that was so close to my heart and the hearts of my team members, and somehow translated that beautifully into an image.

I was eager to get those images out in a big way and leverage their impact. We placed ads on the back of the *New York Times* Sunday Style section, on New York City billboards, and in every fashion magazine geared toward young women at a time when magazines were king.

About a year after launching those print ads and running several different versions of them, we released our one and only "big head" commercial. It featured two models from the print ads using a stop-motion animation technique that created disjointed movement. Then we added this cool, jittery music that somehow complemented the commercial's funky style and overall vibe. That commercial is now in the permanent collection at the Museum of Modern Art, which is pretty unbelievable. A clip from it also appeared years later in *The Wolf of Wall Street*.

We knew we were on to something and kept going with new big-head ads for each season, but after the first year some people on the team wanted to stop, worried that the ads would get stale. As a public company, we had a board of directors, and one of my jobs was to recruit members to join the board. I'd been careful to surround myself with people I trusted. Instead of just choosing people who knew about shoes or fashion, I often offered board seats to people from outside the industry who were sharp and who I knew would keep us honest.

One of those people was Charles Koppelman, a longtime executive in the music business who always wore a suit and had a cigar in his mouth. At one of our board meetings we were talking about doing away with the big heads, and Charles looked horrified. I thought he was going to flick his cigar right at the marketing folks who were saying that we should move on to something new. "If you kill these ads," he said, dramatically taking a puff of his cigar, "it would be like Walt Disney killing Mickey Mouse."

I was so grateful during this time to have people around me who were loyal and smart and always had the company's best interests at heart. In fact, I'd go so far as to say that company morale was a pillar of our early success. I was almost forty years old by then and still single. My relationships always faltered, and I thought I would never get married. But I was OK with that because my team was my family.

Obviously, it was different than a traditional family. It was also much bigger. We were growing rapidly, and around this time I hired Rhonda

Brown, a former executive from Macy's and Lord & Taylor, to be our president and chief operating officer. This was a big hire for us. But as we grew, I did my best to hold onto the same familial vibe we had shared when it was just Wendy, Arvind, and me shipping out shoes and joking around in the back of the SoHo store.

Make no mistake. We worked crazy hours, and I got so heated that I yelled often and wasn't above throwing things. I once nearly grazed an intern's forehead with a four-inch stiletto, and for years, there was a dent in my office wall right next to my desk where I'd thrown the phone in anger so many times. I know, I know. It's terrible. For the record, that dent was covered up years ago and hasn't returned.

Like a temperamental father, I tried to compensate for my outbursts with lots of positive reinforcement and good times. Our annual holiday party was always a huge blowout with steak and lobster and plenty of champagne. The team looked forward to it every year. And we found other excuses to celebrate. My former driver, David, who was now running our Secaucus warehouse, traveled home to Peru to get his green card, and when he returned, I surprised him with a big sheet cake decorated with an image of the American flag.

That same year, one of the guys on our sales team lost his mom, and I chartered a bus to take the staff to the funeral in the middle of the week. It was a somber event, but we all enjoyed one another's company on the bus ride, and he was so grateful that we had shown up for him. This all sounds corny to me now, but it was part of my effort to make these people feel special, as though they were a valuable part of growing this young company into something meaningful. Because they were.

And my team responded in kind, lovingly making fun of me whenever they had the chance. In the early years, Wendy started dressing up like me every year for Halloween. This costume was easy because I wore the same outfit every day, almost like a uniform: a white button-down shirt, jeans, and penny loafers, of course with a baseball hat on my head.

I do the same thing now except that I have swapped the button-down for a white T-shirt. Wendy donned this uniform every Halloween, and eventually the entire team copied her. It was hilarious to walk into the office every year on October 31 and find hundreds of people all dressed like me.

Those people had nothing to do with Jordan Belfort or Stratton Oakmont or any of my poor choices. Steve Madden the company was always completely legitimate and run 100 percent by the books. This was ultimately proven to be true.

Steve Madden the man was another story. The mistakes I made were all related to my private finances and my personal life, not my business. But my biggest fear was that those poor choices would end up hurting the company and the livelihoods of the people who'd been working by my side for years to build it into something that was worth being proud of.

At the same time that I was so busy creating this makeshift family, my own family was rapidly deteriorating. By then, John had divorced his first wife and married a young woman named Sherri with her own substance abuse issues, and their life together seemed chaotic and unsustainable. The wheels had fallen off his charmed life, which I had envied for so long.

Until then, John had always maintained his charming façade. Alcoholism is a progressive disease, and now I started to see signs that the drinking had changed him more than I had realized. His clothes went from impeccable to sloppy, and suddenly he looked decades older than he had just a year or two before.

Luke was now running our Florida warehouse, though he showed up to work drunk most days. It was painful to see how far he had fallen. I was still battling my own addiction and would slip again. But since my dad had passed away, I had tried to be the leader of the family. I supported my mom and our extended family however they needed and had bought my mom a new house in Florida and a car. When a childhood friend of hers was in trouble, I bailed her out. I wasn't consciously trying to redeem myself for being such a disappointment when I was a kid, but on some level, I suppose that's exactly what I was doing.

Ironically, when Danny and Jordan were arrested in the fall of 1998, I heard it from my mom first. She called me from Boca and said, "I hear they're talking." I didn't know where she could have heard that, but I had no doubt that it was true. Danny was in jail and Jordan was out on bail, and they were each facing up to twenty-five years in prison if convicted. I had heard that the government had threatened to also indict Jordan's wife, Nadine, if he didn't cooperate.

Soon after, I went golfing at Engineers Country Club on Long Island's North Shore with Bryan Herman from Monroe Parker and a couple other guys. In the middle of our game, Bryan started talking about Jordan and the rumors going around that he was cooperating. "The government's been asking me a lot of questions," he told me. "I wanted to fill you in."

Right away, I had a strange feeling that something about this conversation was off. "Oh, yeah?" I asked nonchalantly, taking my swing, and did my best to avoid talking to Bryan for the rest of the day.

Within weeks, I heard from many other people that Jordan and Danny were already cooperating with the feds, corroborating against thirty or more other people. I was certain that I was one of them. The idea terrified me. Had Jordan been wearing a wire at the Plaza that day when he came to talk to me about the shares? Was Bryan wearing one at Engineers? Had I accidentally said something incriminating during one of those conversations?

These questions kept me up at night. They led me more than once to call a doctor and beg for pills, claiming that I was in pain. The idea of going to prison pushed me to the edge. It was my greatest fear in life. How could I possibly survive that?

Through it all, though, my focus was on the company. If anything was going to happen to me, I wanted the business to be as strong as possible so it could withstand the blow. We opened more stores, launched new lines, and continued marching our way forward.

I kept busy with these plans and went to meetings when I could force myself to go. Sometimes I golfed on the weekends with my brother John, but more often I was at our SoHo store. Sometimes I'd be there on a Sunday working the floor and think, *What a loser you are! What am I doing here?* But the truth is there was nowhere else I'd rather be.

From 1998 to 2000, we celebrated many big successes as a company while I waited in agony for the axe to fall. More celebrities started wearing our shoes, and it felt like my fifteen minutes of fame was going on its tenth hour. These were the years that Britney Spears and Christina Aguilera came onto the music scene, and they both wore our shoes, as did Janet Jackson, the Spice Girls, and all the other hot young stars.

At the same time, we began licensing handbags, sunglasses, hosiery, outerwear, jewelry, and other accessories, and were busy planning the launch of our men's collection. For years, we'd been grappling with the question of how to appeal to the slightly older women who didn't identify with our brand. At around this time, we finally decided to create a new line called STEVEN that would be geared toward women in their thirties and forties.

I avoided thoughts about how the past might affect my future by focusing on the now, introducing anywhere from ten to fifteen new shoe designs a week. Our sales in 1999 hit one hundred sixty-two million dollars. We opened our fiftieth store in the United States that year. And we hadn't even peaked yet, or crashed and burned.

07
HEEL

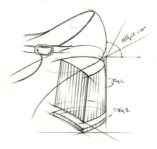

heel • the thick piece of leather or rubber that's attached to the sole of a shoe to raise and support the back of the foot. dress shoes tend to have a separate heel piece, which can be replaced if necessary.

At about six o'clock in the morning on June 20, 2000, about a dozen cops and FBI agents armed with loaded machine guns and decked out in full riot gear burst into my apartment building with the intention of indicting me on federal charges of securities fraud and money laundering. They pounded on the door to my apartment on Mercer Street until someone answered. But that someone wasn't me. I was asleep upstairs the whole time.

About three years earlier, I had rented a second apartment in the same building I'd been living in since the 1980s. The first apartment was on the twenty-first floor, and I moved up to the twenty-sixth floor. John's oldest son, Shawn, had recently moved to New York, and I let him stay in the other apartment while he worked for the company setting up our early web presence.

I wish I could have seen Shawn's face when he opened the door that morning. To his credit, he simply told the officers, "He doesn't live here anymore." They had no clue that he was my nephew or that I was still in the same building. They left, and I slept right through Shawn's frantic phone call and the dozens of other calls that followed as Shawn tried to reach someone who could get in touch with me to tell me what was going on. It was probably the best night's sleep I would get for several more years. I woke up maybe an hour later to roughly forty texts all telling me to get the hell out of the building, because I was about to be indicted.

I jumped out of bed, threw on a pair of jeans and an old, ratty T-shirt, and snuck out the back of the building through the freight elevator. On the way, I called Peter and told him what had happened. "Meet me at Ronny's place, and I'll get Joel," he told me calmly. Ronny was a friend of Peter's, and Joel was my lawyer. I raced to Ronny's office, and within an hour, Peter and Joel came to get me and take me to federal court to surrender.

It was a grueling, painful day, but for months I had known it was coming. When the government went public in the fall of 1999 with the fact that the principals from both Stratton Oakmont (Danny and Jordan) and Monroe Parker (Bryan Herman) were cooperating as witnesses for the government against dozens of people who had committed illegal acts, Peter had helped me find a lawyer, Joel Winograd, in case one of those people was me.

Things were looking bad for the Strattonites, and not just Danny and Jordan. At around the same time, my old friend Dean was arrested for stock fraud along with three other former Stratton brokers. Dean had worked at Stratton until it closed, and we had remained close friends and golfing buddies throughout the years. He called me on the day of his arrest, and I went down to the courthouse with a two-hundred-fifty-thousand-dollar bond so he could make bail.

Dean was still out on bail waiting for a court date when, right around Christmas, the prosecutors asked Joel to bring me in for a meeting. Peter drove us down to the federal building. A few years earlier, I had asked him to join the Steve Madden board of directors, and he was no longer my sponsor because of the conflict of interest. But he was still one of my closest friends.

Joel and I sat around a table in a dimly lit, cement-walled room with about four or five prosecutors, serious-looking guys in worn suits who went through a list of everything they allegedly had on me. "We know that you participated in the manipulation of twenty-nine initial public offerings," one of them told me, "including your own."

"That's absurd," Joel said. He was a big guy with white hair in his sixties who was a former district attorney in Brooklyn. He'd been around the block and gave off the perfect mix of authority and brashness for a defense attorney. "You have no evidence of any of this."

"These charges can carry a sentence of up to twenty-five years," another one of the guys said, looking directly at me. "Think about that. How would you like to go away for that length of time?"

"Don't be ridiculous," Joel blustered. "He's not going anywhere. My client is completely innocent."

There was some hope that if we protested enough, or at least posed like we were going to fight the allegations against me, they would drop the whole thing. After all, I knew plenty of guys who were neck deep in dirty shit and never got into any trouble. So, the idea was to insist that I was innocent and they were wasting their time, hoping they'd choose to focus instead on someone else.

There was a pause. Then one of the guys, the good cop, I suppose, jumped in. "Look, we want to help you avoid that kind of sentence," he said. "Is there anything you can give us? You must know people who are doing illegal things. You can protect yourself and make some cases for us."

I had sensed that this moment was coming. Without even giving it much thought, I knew what my response would be: There was no way I was going to wear a wire or cooperate with the government or any of that shit. To this day, people look at me funny when I say this. They don't understand why I didn't just wear the wire to save my ass. And, look, maybe if I really had been facing twenty-five years, my decision would have been different. But Joel had already assured me that, even with the worst possible outcome, I would end up serving much less time than that, so it just didn't seem worth it. As terrified as I was about going to prison, I would rather take my medicine than go through all the trouble of becoming a rat.

Then they pulled out the big guns. "Steve, it's bad news all around if you can't help us out," the prosecutor continued, looking truly sorry for me. He was convincing. "We have several key witnesses who are testifying in court against you, including the principals of both Stratton Oakmont and Monroe Parker." *Bastards. I knew it.* "That will be damning either way, but we'll go to bat for you with the judge if you cooperate with us."

Joel and I sent our heads shaking again as Joel insisted that I had nothing to worry about, because I hadn't done anything wrong. "We're gonna fight this tooth and nail," Joel said as we got up to leave. "It'll be a big waste of time and money for you to pursue this. You know who the bad guys are here. Worry about them instead."

But I wasn't innocent. I knew that by then, and I know it now. I was guilty and foolish and greedy and obsessed; call it addicted if you're feeling generous. And I was willing to pay my price before getting involved in cooperating with the government.

Looking back, it was the right decision. But I don't want to make it sound like it was this great moral thing or that I'm some kind of martyr. It was just something that I didn't want to do. And while I bitterly resented the guys who were lining up to tell on me, I also understood why they did it. The government is very tough. They can break anyone, and Jordan and Danny were facing serious time in prison.

I left that meeting hoping for a miracle but knowing how infrequently miracles occur. I climbed into Peter's car feeling despondent. "They want me to cooperate, wear a wire," I told him.

"What did you say?" Peter pulled away from the courthouse, avoiding a small group of photographers standing around, hoping to see a celebrity. I pulled my baseball hat down, trying to cover my eyes. They hadn't recognized me.

"Nah, I'm not doing all that," I told Peter. "Besides, you know me. With my ADHD, I'd be a terrible witness. I can hardly remember any of the things I've done. Maybe I really *am* innocent." I elbowed Peter in the ribs, trying to make light of the situation. He just laughed, and we headed back to the office. We never spoke about the meeting or the possibility of wearing a wire again.

For the next six months, I went to the office and attended a meeting every day, focusing completely on the company and on maintaining my sobriety. Besides Peter and Joel, no one even knew that I had met with the feds, so my indictment on that June morning in 2000 was as shocking to everyone else as it was expected by me.

I had been indicted in two districts because of my dealings with both Stratton (the Eastern District, in Brooklyn) and Monroe Parker (the Southern District, in Manhattan), so on the day of my indictment I had to surrender in two separate courts. Ugh, what a day that was. First, we had to go down to the federal courthouse in Brooklyn, right under the Brooklyn Bridge. I didn't know what to expect, but this was not it. They cuffed me, read me my rights, and put me in a cell in the back of the courthouse. I sat there on a hard, grey bench with my head down, not knowing what would happen next. Joel had assured me that everything would be OK, but I had no idea what was going on outside of that jail cell. Finally, a cop called my name and took me into the courtroom where Joel was already waiting. When he saw me, he patted my shoulder and asked if I was OK. All I could do was nod.

The judge entered, and a cop read all the charges against me. Within minutes, the judge set the terms of my seven-hundred-fifty-thousand-dollar bail. The next two hours or so were a blur as Joel worked on making arrangements to get me out of there. My friends really showed up for me, and I was grateful. Eddie Lama put up money for my bond, and Sammy Schwartz, who had been working for me as a sales executive since 1992, put up his house. I also put up my own house in the Hamptons, which I'd bought just a few years earlier.

With all of that settled, I was finally free to go. But first I had to do it all over again in Manhattan. So, it was back to the federal court in downtown Manhattan, back in cuffs, back in a jail cell, and then back before a judge. They gave me a tentative trial date, but it was all really for show. I was already pretty sure that I would plead out and end up having to go to prison for at least some length of time. I could see the future clearly, and it played out pretty much exactly how I imagined it would. But first we had to go through the motions.

Because of federal sentencing guidelines, Joel had already explained to me that if I went to trial and was found guilty, I'd get a much longer sentence than I would if I settled. By the way, this is why so many innocent people end up pleading out, but that's another story. I didn't want to put the company or myself through a trial. As it was, the company was taking a hit for my stupid mistakes. I wasn't aware of it as I sat in those jail cells, but as soon as the news of my indictment broke, the price of Steve Madden stock plummeted from a value of thirteen dollars and thirteen cents a share the day before to only five dollars and fifty cents a share. It was devastating.

As I was surrendering, Arvind was gathering all of our confused and worried employees in our conference room and telling them that we'd face the problem at hand and make sure everything was going to be OK. Meanwhile, Rhonda immediately began doing damage control, issuing statements, and making media appearances about the strength of the company and the illegitimacy of the claims against me.

Leaving the courthouse, I had to walk through a little park to get to the car, and this time a big group of reporters were following me, screaming out questions and sticking their microphones in my face. *"Are you guilty?" "Did you flip stocks for Jordan Belfort?" "Did you help manipulate your own stock?" "What will happen to the company if you go to prison?"*

I was wearing a baseball hat, as usual, and one of the reporters kept asking me what the symbol on the hat meant. I didn't even know what hat I was wearing. It was just something I had grabbed that morning. I kept up my pace, repeating the phrase, "No comment." I was shocked that they had all bothered to be there. I still didn't think of myself as a celebrity, but the news of my indictment was getting around, and it was a pretty big story.

Instead of heading straight to the office, I went downtown. Normally, with the company in crisis, I would be the one at work leading the charge, reassuring everyone that it was all going to be OK. But that night, I let my team handle the emergency and headed to a meeting I was scheduled to chair down at Perry Street, where I'd first gotten sober.

In the program, chairing a meeting is considered an honor, and that night it felt especially true. It had been a long, punishing day, probably the worst one of my life at that point. But what I felt as I led that meeting was an immense sense of gratitude. I had so much to be grateful for: a team that had my back and was sticking by me, friends who were willing to put up their homes against my freedom, and this roomful of people who had helped me stay mostly clean for more than a decade. For just a brief moment, everything felt right.

And then it was back to business as usual, which was eerie after going through the indictment. Yes, the company was in damage-control mode, but we were also still in the midst of a major growth phase. I had no intention of letting a guilty plea or a potential prison sentence do anything to stop that. My team had rallied around me, Joel was optimistic about the possibility of a minimal sentence, and for the moment I was free to focus completely on work, which became a healthy distraction.

We opened fifteen new stores in 2000, branching out more and more on the West Coast. We had also been planning to launch a line of men's shoes for a while, and now the time was right. Not long before, I had met a man named Harry Chen who owned a small men's shoe company, which we folded into the business as Steve Madden Men's.

We announced the new men's line in the fall of 2000, and then fully launched in the spring of 2001. The announcement was met with a ton of skepticism within the industry that I would know how to design for men or market to men or whatever bullshit. As always, we just focused on putting out a good product, and the response from the people who mattered—the customers—was huge, adding tremendous sales growth to the company right away.

I was especially proud of the success of the men's line because it had so little to do with me. That may sound ironic, but I knew by then that I could make great shoes. I was experienced at creating a fantastic product at an accessible price and still making a profit. It was a huge rush every time, but it was something I knew how to do. The ability to choose the right people for a project and motivate them spoke more to my effectiveness as a leader, which was meaningful to me.

As we were growing and creating and trying to push forward, Joel was going back and forth with the prosecutors, working through the investigation and filing the proper motions. It was amazing to me how mundane it all was, and there were constant delays and complications.

Danny had gotten in trouble for another case of insider trading in the midst of his cooperation, and was suddenly a bad witness for the government. They couldn't take his testimony if he was being indicted on another case. The prosecutors told Joel that they had replaced Danny with another witness who was testifying against me, but that didn't make sense. Who could that new witness be?

I was flying to Los Angeles to do some personal appearances in our new stores and meet with vendors out there, and this question was still bothering me. "We already know they have Belfort, Danny, and Bryan," I said to Peter, who was sitting next to me on the plane. "Danny's out, but who else could be ratting on me?"

Peter thought about it for a moment as I stared out the tiny window. "You don't think it could be Dean, do you?"

I turned my head to look at Peter with an expression that said, *You're crazy.* Sure, on one hand, it made sense. Dean knew all about my dealings

Me, my dad, and my brother John when I was about four years old

Me and my dad at Niagara Falls

Me and my mom at Niagara Falls

Learning to play golf at around age 6

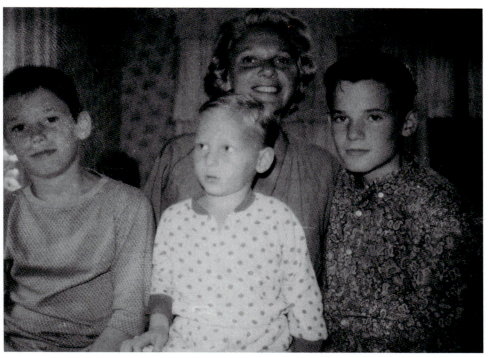

Me, my mom, and my brothers. Luke is to my right and John to my left.

Practicing my golf swing at age 15

Me in Junior High with my friend Marc Mayo

Me in High School

Me and my crew of High School buddies. Danny Porush is to my right.

My brother Luke the hippie in 1973

Cleaning up at the first Steve Madden store in 1993

With Arvind in the late 1990s

Shoes have always been my greatest love...

With the team in the factory in the early 2000s

Me and Wendy the year we got married

With Stevie and Jack

With Wendy, Stevie, Jack, and Goldie

Me, my mom, and my brothers, one of the last times we were all together

With the team in the factory in 2009

Ringing the bell at NASDAQ in 2010

With the team after ringing the NASDAQ bell in 2010

Me, Eddie Lama, and Peter Migliorini

Our VP of Sales, Phil Pine, surrounded by our shoes

With Stevie in the Hollywood Hills, Christmas 2018

With Mary Kate and Ashley Olsen

With Kendall and Kylie Jenner

Me and Nicole Sherzinger from the Pussycat Dolls

With Katy Perry

With Cardi B

With Ja Rule

with Stratton and certainly had plenty of dirt against me. And it was no secret that he was in trouble. But we had known each other since we were little kids, and he had always been one of my best friends. I'd gotten him sober, given him a two-hundred-fifty-thousand-dollar bond, and done him plenty of other favors over the years.

"I just bailed him out last year," I told Peter, waving his thought away with my hand. "There's no way he'd cooperate against me."

It turned out that I was wrong. Joel told me later that Dean was indeed a government witness against me. I was stunned. We heard that the information Dean ended up giving the feds mostly amounted to a character assassination—details of our wild drug use back in the day and all the stupid shit we used to do when we were kids. It didn't really hurt me in terms of my case, but on a personal level it was incredibly painful.

I don't hold a grudge against Danny or Jordan today. They were facing real time, and although I don't like it, I understand why they did what they did. But Dean was different. That one stung. Still does.

Soon, Joel had reached a plea deal with the prosecutors for somewhere between forty-one to fifty-one months in prison along with some hefty fines. I was devastated. The fines were one thing, but the idea of going to prison terrified me. There was nothing I could do, though. I had to pay the price for what I had done.

This was a low point for me. Friends had turned against me, and I might lose the one good thing I had done in my life, all for a stupid, greedy mistake. The company was my whole life. Without it, I literally had nothing. It was who I was, and at the same time, it was my source of redemption that cleansed my prior fuck-ups, of which there were many. And now this one big fuck-up threatened to ruin it all.

As depressed as I was, knowing that I would be going away for some time motivated me to shore up the company. It had to be as solid and strong as possible to withstand my absence. In addition to prison time and fines, part of my sentence would likely be a ban from acting as an officer or director of a publicly traded company, which meant I would have to step down as the CEO of Steve Madden.

The most obvious solution was to sell the company. This would offer some stability while I was away and hopefully allow me to come back to work after my release. Charles Koppelman, who was now the chairman of our board of directors, led the charge of working out a potential sale. Soon, we had two real offers. The first was from Nautica, which at the time was a strong and rapidly growing company in its own right. Harvey Sanders was the CEO of Nautica, and he swooped in with an aggressive offer to buy the company for seventeen dollars a share when I was at my most despondent about going to prison and afraid of losing everything.

I was in favor of the sale, and Charles began negotiations, but right away the process was strained. First, Sanders insisted that part of the deal was that I couldn't stay with the company or come back after my release. I was a bad apple, and they didn't want me spoiling the bunch. In my lowest moments, I would have agreed to this. But at the same time that Sanders wanted a clean break from me, he argued that the company was worthless without me. We tried to position Rhonda as someone who could take over for me, but they weren't happy with that solution, either.

Sanders and Koppelman went back and forth, and eventually the whole deal fell apart. Thank God. Nautica was hot in the 1990s, but their sales started sliding downhill soon after. Two years after our deal went bust, it was sold to the VF Corporation, which sold it again in 2018 after years in the red. I was disappointed when our sale fell through, but now I'm so grateful that it did.

Soon after, we went through a similar process with Kenneth Cole. They offered to buy us and then went through the same motions as Nautica, wanting the company but not me. The truth is that there was no company without me in those days. As soon as these potential buyers scratched the surface, they could see that in my absence Steve Madden was nothing but an empty shell.

This is not the case today. In fact, the very process of me letting go has strengthened the company more than I ever could have imagined. Before I went away, I was consumed by fears that the company would fall apart without me, so I built a deeper team of people as reinforcements. On top of that, my existing team stepped up and stopped being so dependent on me. The irony is that if I hadn't gone away, we wouldn't be the company that we are today. And, of course, I wouldn't be the man I am today, either.

But I couldn't have predicted any of this then. All I knew was that I had to step aside as CEO even before my sentencing so there would be some consistency within the company and no reason for Wall Street to panic when I was inevitably sentenced to several years in prison.

Rhonda was the most likely candidate for the job of CEO. The people on Wall Street loved her because she knew how to speak their language, and by then she had been the president and COO of the company for several years. But just because she was the obvious choice on paper didn't mean she was the right one. While I was in prison, I needed to have someone in that role whom I trusted implicitly, who understood and shared my values on a gut level. It's a total cliché to compare it to trusting someone with my child, but that's exactly how it felt.

A childhood friend of mine named Jamie Karson had been on our board of directors for a while and was a partner at a law firm that had done some legal work for the company. It wasn't a traditional move to hire a lawyer as CEO, but I'm not a traditional guy. Jamie was like a brother to me. He wasn't a shoe guy, and he had never run a big business before, but he understood the spirit of the company better than almost anyone other than me, and I knew that with him in charge while I was away, Steve Madden would be the same company with the same *je ne sais quoi* when I got out.

Besides, the retail fashion business was in Jamie's blood. His parents were both in the fashion business, and Jamie had been involved in running their company early in his career. Since then, he'd done a lot of legal work for retailers. So, it wasn't completely outside the realm of normalcy to hire Jamie as CEO. And most important to me, I trusted him completely, Wall Street trusted him, and our employees trusted him. They knew we were so close that Jamie being in charge was the next best thing to having me there.

When I chose Jamie for the job over Rhonda, she left to become president and CEO of Nine West, one of our biggest competitors. I was sorry to see her go, but I was able to move forward knowing without a doubt that the person in the driver's seat had my back.

On May 2, 2001, I announced my resignation as chief executive of Steve Madden, naming Jamie as my replacement. I would stay on board as creative and design chief of the company. It was devastating, but I was in planning mode and didn't bother stopping to reflect on how painful it was in the moment.

Three weeks later, David drove me to the courthouse. He was now running our warehouse in New Jersey, but he still acted as my driver once in a while. And thank goodness he now had a nicer car. Before I got out in front of the court, he turned to look at me. "Are you going to be OK, Steve?"

I shoved him in the shoulder, but he was so much more solid than I was that he barely budged. "Get out of here," I told him jovially. "I'll be fine."

It was the same line I'd been using with my team ever since the indictment. I knew how important it was to put on a brave face so they would feel strong and confident to keep the business afloat while I was away. I told them over and over that I would be fine, that I had this, that without a wife and kids, going away for a couple years would be no big deal for me. Inside, I was more terrified than I had ever been in my life. But I sold them on the idea that I was OK with the same passion I'd used to sell the Marilyn out of David's car ten years earlier.

As an entrepreneur, you're always selling. It's not enough to just create something, no matter how amazing that product may be. You have to sell it, but that's not enough either. You also have to constantly sell people into your dream and sell your employees to get them amped up. That's what I'd been doing all along as I built the business, and that's what I did now to make sure it would withstand my time in prison.

On May 24, 2001, I entered my guilty plea before Judge Kimba Wood in Manhattan and later before Judge John Gleeson in Brooklyn. Under our agreement, which was covered by both courts, I faced a prison sentence of anywhere between forty-one to fifty-one months. Plus, I owed roughly eleven million dollars in restitution, fines, and fees, and was barred from serving as an officer or director of any publicly traded company for seven years. They set a court date for me to be formally sentenced in September 2001.

But, of course, something happened that September. I was in Minnesota on September 11 for a target vendor day playing golf. I was at the hotel watching the news when the first plane hit. My first thought was not of terrorism, but of the time back in 1945 when a military plane struck the Empire State Building. My father had been a young man in the fabric business then, and his office was in the Empire State Building. He was in the building the day of that freak accident, and while a handful of people were sadly killed, it wasn't an act of terrorism or national disaster. When I first heard the news, I assumed this was the same type of thing, but obviously I was wrong.

When the second plane hit, I immediately extended my stay at the hotel and started calling around to make sure everyone was OK. Wendy lived downtown in Tribeca and had debris in her apartment, but she had evacuated and was alright. Other friends and team members had crazy stories of walking over the Brooklyn Bridge or sleeping on friends' couches because they couldn't make it home. But they all seemed to be OK.

It was a harrowing day, but I felt somewhat disconnected from the tragedy because I wasn't there. Three days later, I was able to fly home. Before landing at JFK, the plane turned around and flew up the Hudson River, and I saw it, the hole in the ground, and no longer felt disconnected.

A few days later, Joel called me. "Your hearing has been delayed," he told me. I exhaled a big sigh of relief. I knew the inevitable was coming, and there was a part of me that wanted to just get it over with. After all, the sooner you go in, the sooner you get out. But there was a much stronger instinct to delay the whole thing for as long as humanly possible.

All the waiting and the back and forth did eventually get to me, though. At work, I pretended I was fine, but inside I was hurting, terrified, and just plain worn out. I had worked hard to stay sober throughout my indictment, the negotiations, and the plea deal, even as I stepped aside as the CEO of the company I'd been building for so long. But it all got to be too much, and one day that fall, shortly after 9/11, I threw in the towel and found myself calling yet another doctor and asking him for pills. By the time I went in for my sentencing hearing in December, I was completely messed up on a fistful of painkillers.

We had already reached a deal with the prosecutors, but we needed both judges to sign off on it. This time, when I got out of the car at the federal court in Manhattan, there were a ton of reporters swarming the car, knocking into me trying to get a shot. "Relax, I'll let you take a picture," I told them, trying to exude the calm and confidence I was really lacking. "I'm not hiding." The photographers continued snapping at me until I stepped inside the court.

I sat with Joel as we waited for Judge Kimba Wood to appear on the bench. Directly behind me were maybe a dozen of my closest friends and team members. I was scared. I knew what was going to happen, but it was still terrifying for a prison sentence to go from an inevitability to a reality.

Judge Wood sat down at her bench, and Joel had a chance to make one last statement, extolling my virtues and defending my bad choices. "He has led a wonderful life and has gone astray," he said, going on to explain that I suffered from addiction and that this had contributed to my poor decision-making. He described my years of work with the program, the organizations I had given money to, and the people I had helped along the way. "My client has fallen from grace, Your Honor," Joel said sadly, "and he is deeply remorseful."

For years, celebrities had been wearing my shoes and calling me a creative genius. I had won style awards and industry accolades. I never took any of that seriously. But hearing someone praise me in this context was too much. My shoulders began to shake as I fought back tears. When I couldn't hold them in any longer, I buried my face in my hands.

Then it was Judge Wood's turn to speak, and what she said was shocking. "We're going to adjourn this," she said. "You won't be sentenced today." She told us that she wanted to study the law thoroughly on her own to see if there was a legal rational to divert from the federal sentencing guidelines if my addiction had played a role in my crimes. I was stunned. The irony wasn't lost on me that my addiction might end up saving me when I was high at that very moment. "Thank you, Your Honor," I managed to say.

As soon as Judge Wood left the bench, Joel clapped me on the shoulder. "This is great," he said. Everyone around me was celebrating, but I could barely comprehend what was happening. It was too much to take in.

The next few months were filled with hope, a few desperate efforts to stop taking pills, and more slips and falls. Judge Wood asked us to present legal briefs justifying a reduced prison sentence, so we hired a slew of additional lawyers to help make our case. Finally, they submitted their briefs, and we got another court date for the spring.

Going back to court was like having déjà vu all over again. I sat in Judge Wood's courthouse for the last time, hopeful, terrified, and, sadly, high. As soon as she sat down at the bench, I knew what her answer was going to be. And sure enough, she finally delivered the blow. "I am bound by our sentencing guidelines," she said with no emotion in her voice. "There isn't a compelling enough reason to downwardly depart."

I was numb. All that time. All that hope. And yet, here we were. Later that day, I went before Judge Gleeson, and he confirmed the sentence:

forty-one months in a federal penitentiary. That's three and a half years. Three Christmases. Three birthdays. A lifetime in the fashion industry. And for what? Money. It all seemed so foolish to me now. So incredibly stupid. But the time for regret was over. I had to pay for what I had done.

That entire summer was a blur. I spent every day in the office selling my team on the idea that everything was going to be fine and making a few more key hires to fill in any lingering gaps. And every night, I got blasted in my apartment and hid away from the rest of the world.

Judge Wood had allowed me to self-surrender, which meant I had to show up at the prison on my own. I was set to do so in September. As the summer spun by me, I knew I had to get clean. There was no way I could survive my first days in prison while detoxing from opioids. But as hard as I tried, every day I found myself reaching for my pills. I was as helpless as always against their power.

Finally, one Sunday morning in early August, Peter and Eddie and a few other guys showed up in my apartment. "Come on, we're gonna go for a drive," Eddie said. Peter was waiting downstairs in his car, and I got in. I didn't even ask where we were going. I was too messed up and simply too worn out. I just sat in the back seat staring out the window as Peter drove. As soon as we got onto the Saw Mill River Parkway, I knew they were taking me to yet another rehab facility.

I didn't fight it. Honestly, I was relieved that the decision had been taken away from me. Looking back, I'm so grateful to those guys for getting me the help I needed. It was roughly the fifth time I detoxed from opioids. It never gets any easier. But I knew I had to do it one more time.

After I got home, I gathered about twenty members of my team and brought them all out to the Hamptons for a weekend-long sales meeting slash goodbye party. We talked about where we were going as a company and how decisions should be made in my absence. But mostly we just enjoyed being together over bonfires on the beach, dinners out on the patio, and chicken fights in the pool.

I looked at my team that last night, thinking about how lucky I was that they were standing by me through all of this. I had been saying for months that I could do my time because I didn't have a family and kids. But I had grown up with many of these people. Others had been working for me since they were teenagers. These *were* my kids. And no matter how many times I kept telling them that it would be OK, it hurt like hell to leave them.

I went from person to person over the course of the evening, using everything I had in me to make sure they felt secure and capable of moving on without me. By the end of the night, even I believed it. But could I survive without them? I was a lot less sure of that.

And then the next day I was gone.

08
SHANK

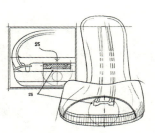

shank • a piece of metal inserted between the sole
and the insole lying against the arch of the foot.

"**T**ake care of Rob Schmertz," I told Jamie as we walked in circles around the lobby of our hotel. Later that morning, I was going to self-surrender at the Eglin Federal Prison Camp, and I took this moment to download my thoughts, concerns, and priorities to Steve Madden's new CEO.

Since 1997, Rob had been my number-two guy. We partnered on everything: designing the shoes, deciding how our stores should look, and putting together each season's lines. Rob understood me better than almost anyone. And most of all, if Rob told me that he liked a shoe, I knew it would be a hit. There were very few people I could say that about. But like most artistic people, Rob was sensitive, and I knew that in my absence he'd need special care.

My brother John, Jamie, Peter, Mark, and a couple other board members had flown down to Florida with me the day before. Inside, I was terrified. I was doing my best to maintain a calm exterior for the benefit of the other guys, but I'm sure they didn't buy my act. "It's gonna be OK, Steve," Jamie assured me. "We've got it covered. Just focus on getting through this. Eglin won't be so bad."

He was probably right. Eglin was a minimum-security prison on the Eglin Air Force Base in Western Florida, and it had a reputation for being so cushy that the term *Club Fed* was coined to describe it. There were no fences. You could just get up and walk off the prison grounds if you wanted to, though you would face stiff consequences if you were crazy enough to do that. But no matter how comfortable it may have been compared to other facilities, it was still a prison. It was not going to be easy.

My sentence was for forty-one months, but I had gotten into a prison drug and alcohol rehabilitation program. This meant I would attend classes and meetings for nine months inside, and in exchange, eighteen months would be taken off my sentence. If everything went according to plan, my sentence would get cut down even further for good behavior. All told, I was looking at more like seventeen months than forty-one. I could handle that, I kept telling myself. I could survive.

The guys drove me over shortly after. Eglin Air Force Base was a huge campus taking up hundreds of square miles where the air force developed and tested all sorts of weapons. It almost looked like a little military city. There were dozens of industrial-looking buildings that I assumed were the testing facilities and dormitories and housing units for military families. The compound even had a golf course that inmates took care of and a bus line to get residents from one end of the complex to the other. The prison was just one small building on the vast grounds. Jamie pulled up outside of it far too soon.

No one could come in with me, and it wasn't the kind of place for long goodbyes. I simply got out of the car as a guard came out to get me. Immediately, my delusions that this place would live up to its nickname were shattered. As I approached the guard, he looked at me with disdain. "Let's go," he said gruffly as he yanked my arms behind me and tightened a pair of cuffs around my wrists. I glanced back at the carful of guys. They looked stricken. I nodded to them once to let them know I was OK before the guard nudged me wordlessly toward the building's entrance.

I don't know exactly what I had expected, that they would escort me to my room like I was checking in at the Hilton? No. As soon as we walked inside the prison, everything changed. The guards made it clear that I was nothing to them. Worthless. They took all of my belongings away from me, even the biography of the Rolling Stones that I had brought with me to read. "You can't bring anything but a bible," a guard said scornfully, tossing my book aside. He threw an orange jumpsuit at me and took me into a tiny washroom to change. Then it was time for a strip search, the horrors of which cannot be overstated.

As we went through the motions of my intake, the guards jostled me about, not really hurting me or anything; just treating me physically and verbally like I was subhuman. I suppose there are plenty of people who support this and believe that if you've committed a crime, you deserve to be treated like garbage. But all this does is harden people who have made mistakes instead of rehabilitating them. We can punish people for their crimes and remain compassionate. I had many more months to learn about all the injustices of our prison system, but my crash course started right away.

When the guards were done with me, they released me onto the grounds. I looked around feeling numb, in shock. The first thing I noticed was that it was quieter than I had imagined. A few guys sat around a picnic table playing cards. A few yards away, I saw a few guys with gardening shears trimming up some hedges. There were also a handful of guards sprinkled around, mostly just staring off into the distance. It was September and still hot, and the Florida air was heavy. I immediately felt myself beginning to sweat in my jumpsuit.

Then out of nowhere a familiar figure approached. For years, Elliot Lavigne and I had been on parallel paths. He was good friends with Jordan Belfort and was another one of his top guys for flipping stocks. I had met Elliot a few times over the years and always liked him, a handsome, silver-tongued fashion executive who probably would have gone on to become a titan in the industry if he hadn't gotten in trouble. Elliot was a former executive at Perry Ellis and had helped build the incredibly profitable FUBU brand when he was CEO of the Jordache Company. But he'd been indicted at around the same time as me on similar charges. Jordan had probably ratted on him too.

"Hey, man," I said as Elliot approached. It was shocking to see someone who was always decked out in the finest Italian suits standing beside me in prison garb. Meanwhile, I always dressed so poorly that I probably looked more fashionable in my orange jumpsuit than I normally did. But I kept the surprise of seeing Elliot like this to myself and shook his hand. "How's it going?" I studied his eyes for signs of shock or trauma, but it was hard to tell, and, anyway, he didn't answer.

"I got your stuff for you," he said instead, handing me a laundry bag.

I peered inside the bag and saw that it held a few necessities. Well, prison necessities: toothpaste, a toothbrush, a bar of soap, and cigarettes. "Thank you," I told him, grateful for the normalcy of a familiar face. "So," I asked him, trying to smile, "am I going to make it? What do I need to know?"

Elliot showed me around the camp. "You'll be fine," he said as we walked into the brightly fluorescent-lit building. "Just keep to yourself and stay out of trouble. If you see some crazy shit going down, head in the other direction." I walked quickly to keep up with Elliot, taking it all in. "Don't talk about what you have on the outside. None of that matters here."

We walked through the barracks, military-style open cubes that each held a set of bunk beds and two small lockers, passing by a guard who looked right through us. "Don't try to be friendly to the guards," Elliot said. "In fact, don't even bother talking to them. If you have to, act deferential. It sucks, but it'll save your ass."

I nodded. "Where is everybody?" I had assumed that the other guys would be inside, but it was just as quiet in here as it was out in the yard.

"Work," Elliot answered. "After breakfast is work straight through until lunch. You'll probably get assigned tomorrow. They let me take a break to come act as your welcoming committee." I smiled for the first time that day. "Most of the guys work off-site on the base in one of the testing facilities. The guys you see around now work on one of the night crews."

We entered a rec room with folding chairs and one television in the corner. A group of young Italian guys sat in the corner with their heads bent close together as they talked. Elliot cocked his head in the direction of the door, and we went back out. "Most of the guys are cool, but stay away from them," Elliot told me quietly with no further explanation.

We moved on to the cafeteria. A couple guys were working in there, mopping the floor. Elliot seemed much happier to see them. "This here's Byron," he said, introducing me to a young black guy. "We call him Belly. And this is Arjan. Guys, this is Steve. He's new." I shook both of their hands. Byron looked like a teenager and was friendly enough. Arjan just nodded at me. He was tough, with a buzzed head and tanned skin that was covered in tattoos.

We chatted for a minute. I learned that Belly was from Louisiana and assessed that Arjan was some kind of Albanian gangster. Then Elliot interrupted. "Alright, man, we gotta go." He had to get back to work, so he walked me over to my cube and left me there. "You'll be OK," he said again before he left. "I'll see you later."

I looked around and imagined myself living here for the next seventeen months. It was so completely unfathomable; it might as well have been seventeen years. The bottom bunk was made with military precision, and the top bunk, which I assumed was mine, had just a flat sheet roughly folded on top. I climbed up there and lay down, staring at the drop ceiling speckled with water spots that I would soon come to memorize. How the hell was I going to survive this?

I didn't know the answer, but a few things were already clear to me. For one, it wasn't going to do me any good to sit around feeling sorry for myself. I had screwed up, just like all the guys in here, and I had to do my time just like they were doing theirs. Maybe there was a way I could use that time to better myself or even to benefit the rest of the population. That would be my secondary goal. But my first goal, I realized, had to be simply getting through it, surviving. That was my full-time job now. Not designing shoes. Not leading a team. Not obsessing about product and speed to market and pricing and production costs and hiring and firing. Just surviving. If I could do all of those things, I told myself, then I could survive this.

"Who the fuck are you?" A mean-looking older guy with a Spanish accent interrupted me.

I hopped down off of the bunk and stuck out my hand. "Oh, hey, man, I'm Steve."

He just gave me a withering look. "Hernando," he said. "And what is this shit?" He gestured to my bunk and the laundry bag of stuff that I'd dropped on the ground.

"I'll get that." I grabbed the laundry bag and started putting the things Elliot had given me away in my locker. But he interrupted me again.

"You gotta keep your shit tight, you hear me?"

I nodded. "Yeah, man, no problem." But I knew I had my work cut out for me. I'd never gotten along with anyone I'd lived with because I was such a mess, and I could be terribly selfish at times. But now a part of my survival would have to be adapting to my surroundings and coming around to a different way of life. I honestly didn't know if I could do it.

The next day, I got assigned to the landscaping crew. A shockingly loud alarm woke us up early, and after a quick and unappetizing breakfast, everyone went off to report to work. "You're out on the golf course," the guard who oversaw the landscaping crew told me. I got into a van with a few other guys, and we spent the entire day mowing the grass and doing other manual labor in the blazing heat.

I thought about all of the golf courses I had played at around the world and the irony that this was my work assignment in prison. But after a couple days, the guard pulled me from the course. "Too much notoriety," was all he told me. I wondered if someone had recognized me and why they thought that me being on the course would be a problem, but I thought better than to ask.

From then on, my job was to work with the regular landscaping crew on the prison grounds. There were maybe twenty of us in all, and we split up in smaller groups that could each fit on one of the golf carts we used to get around. My crew was assigned to work on the sprinkler system, digging up pipes and putting in PVC. It was me, a Mexican guy named Camacho, and Don Keling, a good old boy from Oklahoma. We were an odd group, but we got along, and whenever we could we hung out with Neville, a black guy on the landscaping crew who worked much harder than the rest of us and was always riding around on a big machine mowing the grass.

I never worked out in my life before prison, but I understood right away why prisoners are known for spending so much time working out and lifting weights. For one thing, it doesn't hurt to be strong and big so people don't mess with you. And it helps to pass the time. But most important, it's one of the few positive things that you can do on the inside. Working out gives you an element of control in an environment in which you have so little autonomy. You can't control what you eat or who you live with or what time you wake up in the morning, but you can decide to lift a weight and work a muscle to make it bigger. And that feeling of self-determination is priceless.

Pretty soon I was working out every day. There was a weight pile, as we called it, in a little shack out on the grounds. My crew would report to work each morning, put our stuff in our golf cart, and instead of driving around fixing sprinklers, we'd go straight to the weight pile to work out. Sometimes Neville would join us, but most of the time he was working. There was a guard overseeing our little crew, but he was pretty lax and barely paid attention to what we were doing. After our workout, we drove around putting in PVC pipes. Even then, we would mostly sit around shooting the shit and then quickly act busy if we saw a guard approaching.

The rest of the day outside of work soon followed its own routine. Breakfast, work, lunch, more work, and then I'd read for a while before dinner. There was a little library in the prison, and I rediscovered my love of reading, which really saved me by giving me something bigger than myself to think about. After dinner, I'd play cards with Elliot and some of the other guys or write letters to people back home, and then it was lights out. I'd climb up to my bunk and thank the heavens that I'd survived one more day.

Ever since I was a little boy, I've had the ability to go somewhere else in my mind, like I'm watching a movie of myself living an alternate life. Lying on my bunk, I watched movie after movie of myself as a father, husband, professional golfer, or businessman. In prison, I thought a lot about being a father. This was something I had always wanted, and now I worried that I would miss out on it because I was spending some of my prime years locked up. But the moments I created in my mind felt so real at times that the prison walls and even the confines of reality weren't quite so limiting.

It sounds pretty good as I'm retelling it, and on some days, it was actually OK. I followed Elliot's advice from day one, and I got along with the other guys and really enjoyed spending time with them. Don't get me wrong. There were also days that were unspeakably awful. There was the time the group of Italian guys that Elliot had warned me about cornered me and forced me to share an agonizing meal with them. And the time I saw a guy get beaten unconscious over some small perceived slight. But for the most part, the hardest thing about life in prison wasn't actually life in prison. It was the heartbreak of the world moving on without me while I was stuck in there, trapped in this strange limbo. On some days, I thought, *This must be what it feels like to be dead.*

Those feelings peaked, ironically, on the best days of the week, which were visitor days. I was so grateful to have plenty of visitors. My brother John, Peter, Eddie, Jamie, Wendy, Mark, Rob, and other people from the company all took turns coming to visit. Even my mother came to visit me, determined to make the best of a bad situation. I always tried to assure everyone that I was OK and keep our conversations light. For just a moment, it was like being one step closer to home. Of course, the heartbreak came back twice as strong when it was time for them to leave.

I was clean in prison and kept clear of any guys I sensed might have possibly been selling or using drugs. But I did have one last remaining addiction: nose spray. I couldn't breathe through my nose without it and was afraid of suffocating if I couldn't get those drops.

When I arrived at Eglin, I had hoped they would sell my brand of nose spray at the commissary. Unlike many of the other guys, I was lucky to always have plenty of funds in my commissary account. Some of them, like Belly, had nothing. They couldn't even afford to buy a bar of soap. It was shameful, and I wanted to help, but I knew it would get me in trouble if I just started handing out items from the commissary. So, I started asking some guys to do favors for me, and then I paid them with items I bought from the commissary. Belly quickly became my major domo. He did countless errands for me in exchange for the commissary items he couldn't afford to buy.

This system worked pretty well, but the commissary was often out of certain things or suddenly stopped carrying them. And their selection was limited. It turned out they didn't carry nose spray at all, only saline. I told Peter about this during one of our visits, and the next week he poured four bottles of the nose spray into a big container of saline solution and then came to visit me for Friday night services. There was a little chapel on the camp that was used for all sorts of religious purposes. I never went to observe the Sabbath, and Peter wasn't Jewish, but I didn't ask questions when the guard said that he wanted me to meet him in there.

As I sat down, I saw that Peter had left the bottle on the bench right next to him. I quickly grabbed it, stuffed the bottle in the waistband of my pants, and picked up a bible. I glanced over at Peter. He appeared to be reading his bible, looking incredibly devout. Then I noticed that he had it open to the first page, the Christian way. The Jewish bible opens the opposite way, starting in the back. I nudged Peter with my elbow. "The other way, dummy," I hissed at him, gesturing to the book.

Somehow, the months started to pass. After I'd been inside for a few months, Arjan cornered me one night. While I'd become friendly with a lot of the guys by then, and even my cellie, Hernando, was starting to like me, Arjan and I had never spoken much. He had a pair of clippers and buzzed the other guys' hair after dinner in exchange for commissary items, his own little side hustle. The only times we'd spoken were when he'd offered to buzz my hair.

I always declined, but I had to admit my hair was a mess. It was mostly gone by then, and a few years before I'd replaced my long pony-tail with a horrible comb-over that I knew wasn't fooling anyone. Finally, one night, Arjan got in my face. "I'm gonna beat the shit out of you if you don't let me shave your head," he told me.

"OK, OK," I relented, even though I was pretty sure he was joking. I followed Arjan to his bunk, and within moments, my remaining hair was gone, replaced by the bald scalp I still have today.

A lot of guys get tattoos in prison. Sure, sometimes it's gang-related, but beyond that, I understand the urge to make a physical alteration to represent all the ways that prison has changed you. My bald head became that symbol for me, and marked the moment that my transition ended and I became a full-fledged prisoner.

Soon after, a guard approached me at night while I was reading in my bunk. "Let's go, you're switching bunks," he told me. I looked at Hernando. I'd heard that this could happen. They rotated your bunkmates so no two prisoners could get too close and start conspiring or causing trouble. It was hard to believe that they thought of Hernando and me this way, but it was true that we had become friendly over the months. After I quickly packed up my stuff, I held out my hand to Hernando.

"Sorry to see you go, man," he said, shaking my hand and slapping me on the back.

Thinking back, this was one of the proudest moments of my bid. The fact that Hernando had come to like and respect me showed that I had been able to adapt when I wasn't sure that I could. For the first time in my life, instead of doing things my own way, I had worked hard to contort myself and fit in somewhere I never imagined I could belong. This was a skill I continued honing over the next several months.

My next cellie was an older black guy named Tuna who was a Vietnam vet and had been successful in the music business. Tuna was serving a huge amount of time for selling cocaine, but he kept his sense of humor and an optimistic outlook. I loved being around him.

I didn't really talk about my life outside of prison at first, but after a while word about who I was got around. Tuna and some of the other guys started calling me "shoe man." It was a lot better than some of the other nicknames the guys had.

One day, a huge guy named Swole came up to me in the cafeteria. "Shoe man, I need to see you," he said. *Uh-oh*, I thought. Was I about to get my ass kicked? Swole got his name because he was the biggest guy in the joint, and everyone knew to stay away from him. I walked outside with him, bracing myself. "My wife called me about a pair of shoes," he told me. "Some kinda high-heeled boot or something. Can you get them for me?"

I exhaled. "Yeah, man, let me see what I can do."

Swole turned out to be one of the greatest guys I met inside. He taught me his workout routine, which helped me get in better shape, and we became close friends. Like so many of the other black guys I met who were serving serious time, Swole had gotten in trouble for selling drugs. I really connected with these guys. They were cool and smart and, yes, they had made mistakes just like I had. But they taught me so much about the plight of African American men and the problems in their communities.

Look, people of all races make mistakes. But no matter what your politics or personal beliefs are, it's hard to deny the fact that these guys have been dealt a tougher hand than people like me. The drug laws and mandatory sentences are incredibly biased against black people. I met young kids who were serving three hundred months for selling crack that had been flooded into their neighborhoods. Meanwhile, powdered cocaine, which was more popular among white people, carried much lower sentences. Prisons are now warehousing black men at horrifying rates. Do the math, and imagine the havoc this has caused in the African American community.

My political views had been evolving for a while, but this is when I really opened my eyes to new ideas about the way the world works. Besides the unfair drug sentencing, one of the things that struck me was how hard it was for these guys to get jobs outside after their release. I met so many guys who had served their time, gotten released, and then had such a hard time finding a job because of their criminal record that they ended up right back where they had started, selling drugs. Now they were back in prison with even less hope for the future.

The thought didn't fully come together at the time, but the idea hit me that this was something I could help with once I was released, at least in some small way. I knew how lucky I was to have a job, and a pretty good one at that, waiting for me when I got out.

Even inside, I had so much more than most of the other guys, and I looked for small ways I could help. At one point I wrote to my assistant back home and asked her to put five hundred dollars in Belly's commissary account so he could afford to buy necessities. He was a good guy, smart and scrappy, and I suppose in some way he reminded me of myself when I was young. Plus, he had earned that money by doing me favors. To me, it seemed like a perfectly fair transaction.

Most of the time, I didn't think about life outside or shoes or what it would be like when I got out. I just focused on surviving each day as it came. It was ironic, because apparently there were reports in the media that I was running the business from prison, which I wasn't legally allowed to do. During one of his visits, Jamie told me that he'd had to fire one of our salespeople, and in retribution he called a friend at a local New York paper and told him that I was running the company from prison. They ran with the story, and then the *Wall Street Journal* picked it up, causing a bit of a frenzy.

Look, you can run a business buzzing heads or selling commissary items from prison, but you cannot run a shoe company from prison. People could come visit and talk to me about the business, but I wasn't there to create and produce. Whenever my team asked my opinion about something work-related, I told them, "You have to make the call. I'm not there."

The whole thing was a joke. But apparently even the government was taking it seriously. Not long after the WSJ article ran, the SEC called Jamie and asked him about his visits with me. He explained that we mostly gossiped and talked about everything *except* the business. Thankfully, this seemed to appease them.

With that trouble out of the way, I did suggest one thing. If rumors were going to spread about my time in prison, why not give them something to talk about? Jamie took this message to the marketing team, and they started incorporating secret messages into new Steve Madden ads. First, they hid my prisoner ID number in an image of a rock, and then they put a car in one ad with a license plate that read: FREESTEVE. I still hadn't gotten Swole his shoes, so I asked the guys to put his name in the next ad as a little shout-out. It was good fun and reminded me of the way the Beatles used to hide secret messages in their album covers.

At around this time, the board received another offer to buy the company, but now I was strongly against it. I didn't want to give up the one thing outside that I had to go back to. Besides, the light at the end of the tunnel was getting clearer. About thirteen months into my sentence, I was approved for an eight-day furlough. At this point, I had been in the drug and alcohol program for about six months. After returning from my furlough, I'd have three more months followed by a short stint in a half-way house, and then I'd be free. My flights were booked, everything was set, and I was about to have eight glorious days at home with my friends and family. I knew this would help tide me over and give me the strength I needed to withstand the rest of my time away.

Two days before I was set to leave, I was in the rec room playing cards with some of the guys when a guard came over and told me that I needed to report to the lieutenant's office right away. This was new. Over the past year, I'd never been called in like this. But nothing unusual had happened recently, so I wasn't too worried as I walked down the corridor toward the office. Once I was inside, though, I knew something was wrong.

A few guards were gathered in the small office, looking serious and pissed off. The lieutenant sat at his desk. "Did you send five hundred dollars to an inmate named Byron Semian?" he asked me. It took me a second to realize that he was talking about Belly. How had they traced that back to me? "Just tell us the truth," he said, "and we'll go easy on you."

I thought for a moment. Prisoners weren't allowed to send money to one another's commissary accounts. I suppose this was to deter drug dealing and other illegal activity. But I had simply wanted to help Belly, and I foolishly thought they really would go easy on me for that. "Yes, I did," I told them. "He had nothing, and I wanted to help him out."

The lieutenant looked at the other guards. "Alright, let's give him a trial."

Before I knew what was happening, they were setting up a mock trial right there in that office. One guard was assigned to defend me. Another was a makeshift prosecutor. And the lieutenant himself was the judge. The whole time I was wondering if this was some kind of joke. Was this really how they settled things in here? And what was going to happen to me if I was found guilty?

The entire "trial" took all of five minutes. My pseudo-defense attorney pled my case. "He's a good guy," he said to the lieutenant. "He keeps to himself and hasn't gotten in any trouble. We can cut him some slack this time."

"But we don't know why he sent the prisoner that money," the prosecuting guard piped in. "Who knows what they're up to? We can't let things like this slide just because he's some hotshot shoe mogul."

The lieutenant just shook his head. "He's right," he said. "We've got to ship him out." And with that, the guard who just two minutes before had played my defender cuffed me and took me straight to a holding cell in another part of the prison. I was alone with no clue what was happening. They had said they were going to ship me out, but when? And where? Would I even be able to go back to my cube and get my stuff?

The answer was no. They packed up my stuff, and later that night they put me on a van heading to some unknown destination. It would be several more days before I saw sunlight again.

09
THROAT

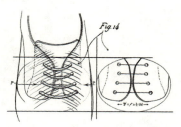

Fig. 14

throat • the front of the vamp next to the toecap. for shoes where the
vamp and quarter panels are one piece, the throat is at the eye-stay.

woke up to the feeling of water lightly misting my face. My body was sore, but I wasn't sure why. It took me a minute to remember where I was, crouched in a fetal position on the hard, cement ground. Then I caught the smell of the liquid that was hitting my face and scurried to my feet, quickly remembering everything.

It wasn't water at all. It was urine, hitting the back of the urinal just inches away and ricocheting onto me. The guy who was relieving himself didn't give a shit, and even if he did, there was nowhere else for him to go. And there were so many of us crammed together in the cell in this Tallahassee detention center that there was nowhere for me to go, either.

I had been here for days. After being shipped out of Eglin, I was taken from one facility to the next, locked in a holding cell each time and then loaded back on a van in the morning. The night I arrived at this particular facility, I couldn't wait to get back on the van the next morning. But that had never happened.

Days later, the only information I had gotten was from the rumors that spread from one cell to the next. This was some kind of way station that held prisoners who were awaiting reassignment. It was a far cry from Eglin. Double rows of cells lined the huge facility with no windows or natural light, and we were kept in there almost the entire day, with trays of barely edible food slipped in at mealtimes.

I did my best to keep to myself and mind my own business. I didn't want any trouble. But when the other guys talked, I listened. Apparently, there were two places where I might be going: the Yazoo County Regional Correctional Facility or the Coleman Federal Correctional Complex. Some of the other guys had been to these places, and the consensus was that I did not want to end up at Yazoo. I spent the next few days blindly praying that I'd get Coleman, not really knowing what that meant and whether it was really any better than the alternative.

Finally, word came down that I was going to Coleman. Because I had been found guilty of sending funds to another inmate, time had been added to my sentence, and I was going from a minimum-security camp to a low-security prison. The whole situation was calamitous, and I cursed myself for making such a stupid mistake. But at that moment, I was mostly just relieved. At least it wasn't Yazoo or another minute at this place. Anything would have been better than that.

It was a long drive to Coleman, and when the van finally pulled up to the compound, I could see how different it was from Eglin right away. For one thing, a wire fence surrounded the entire compound, and that fence was lined with guards armed with machine guns. There was no wandering off this campus.

Later, I'd learn about the other differences, the biggest one being that Coleman had what's called *controlled movement*. At Eglin, when you weren't at work, you could move around the camp however you wanted. Here, you could only move around the compound for ten minutes out of each hour. A bell would ring, signaling that you had ten minutes to get to wherever you wanted to go. Then a second bell ten minutes later meant it was time for lockdown again.

But before I could experience that, I had to go through the horrors of intake for the second time. Then I was sent to solitary confinement.

There was no welcoming committee, no familiar face to greet me with my things. Solitary was about as bad as you might expect, especially because I had no idea how long I was going to be in there or what was waiting for me after I got out. I had nothing with me. I couldn't even read. So, I just tried to stay focused on surviving from one moment to the next in that dank, empty cell.

Finally, after I'd guess about twenty-four hours, a guard came to get me and bring me to my cube. It was the same type of barracks-style layout as Eglin, which brought me some small comfort. But as soon as I met my cellie, that comfort vanished. His real name was Eric, but he was known as Head, and he was the toughest, most institutionalized guy in the joint. Head was big and ripped with long dreads and gold teeth and an enormous chip on his shoulder.

I thought back to Hernando with affection. He was like a pussycat compared to Head. But I had won Hernando over, and I was determined to do the same thing now by adapting in whatever ways I needed to in order to survive.

I wasn't the only one who was afraid of Head. He ran a little shop right out of the cube that sold soda, snacks, toiletries, and all kinds of stuff they had at the commissary, and he was known to be tough. On my first day, I saw guys lining up from all the other dormitories to buy stuff from Head, and I got a sense of what I was dealing with. He was like a mafia boss or an entrepreneur, really, and I respected his hustle as much as I feared his temper.

I was thankful that my commissary account stayed full, and I was able to purchase necessities and even some small comforts like a reading lamp and a small radio. On one of my first nights at Coleman, I was listening to my radio on the top bunk while Head slept on his down below. As I went to switch the radio off, I accidentally knocked it over. There was a huge crash as it bounced off of the rail right behind Head's pillow and landed on the ground.

I held my breath, hoping that somehow it hadn't hit Head. Then in the darkness I saw the shadow of his huge figure rise from the bed to hover over me. He was staring me right in the eye. There was another moment of silence before he spoke. "You tryin' to see me, boy?"

I tried to play it cool. "No, man, I'm sorry about that," I said. He stared at me for another moment and then wordlessly lay back down. I took a deep breath and closed my eyes, asking myself the same question I had asked the first night in Eglin: *How on earth was I going to survive?*

The worst part was that, as part of my reassignment, I had gotten kicked out of the drug and alcohol program, which meant the eighteen months were added back onto my sentence. I could reapply for the program, but I had to be accepted and then start the nine months of the program over from scratch.

Of course, I was desperate to start that nine-month clock ticking as soon as possible, so I reapplied and met with the officer at Coleman who was running the program. It was clear from that first meeting that he hated me on sight. I told him how remorseful I was and how important the drug and alcohol program was for my sobriety, but he blew me off right away. While he let other guys into the program, I kept reapplying and was shut out.

It felt like my world had been turned upside down. Life at Eglin wasn't easy, but I had figured things out, gotten into a routine, and even made friends. Now I had nothing. I had to learn the ropes all over again.

It didn't take me long to figure out that, in this joint, the currency was mackerel. Yes, the fish. The commissary sold bags of dried mackerel that were delicious. I mean, delicious for someone in prison. The guys were working out all the time, and the food they served in the cafeteria never had enough protein to really bulk up. Mackerel was the answer. You could buy a Cup-a-Soup from the commissary, put in hot water, throw a mackerel on top, and have a relatively tasty meal.

But in order to buy mackerel, you had to have money in your commissary account. The guys who didn't have enough got their mackerel from the other inmates in exchange for services or other goods. Thankfully, I always had enough money to buy plenty of mackerel, so before long I cornered the market on this unique form of currency.

This is how I found my way at Coleman, by becoming the mackerel king. I bought ten bags of mackerel at a time (that was the limit) and doled them out in exchange for favors. If I wanted to have my laundry done, I'd give a guy a mackerel. If I wanted to buy cereal to eat for breakfast, I'd give a guy a mackerel. It wasn't quite designing shoes, leading a team, or making deals with Bloomingdale's, but running my little mackerel kingdom helped me get by.

Soon, I was intent on growing my mackerel business. I wanted to have more than ten bags at a time, so I gave some guys money to buy mackerel for me. Yes, this is exactly what I'd just gotten in trouble for at Eglin, but I had to find ways to survive. Head saw this and started expanding his own little store, which brought us closer together. I was still mindful of his temper, but we started getting along and hanging out together in our cube. Eventually we did become friends.

When Head wasn't around or wasn't in the mood to bullshit with me, I'd sit up on my bunk reading books or writing letters to everyone back home. One of the people I wrote to the most was Wendy, because she always wrote back and her letters were so fun and upbeat. I always looked forward to getting a letter or a visit from her. Just like when I'd first hired her, she was always smiling and laughing. Her energy was dynamic and positive, and this translated into her letters, which never failed to put me in a better mood.

It had always been like that between us. Our relationship was strictly professional, but we got a kick out of each other. Unlike when she started working for me, though, the age difference between us now wasn't as big. I know this doesn't add up mathematically, but when we met, Wendy was nineteen and I was in my early thirties. That's a lifetime apart. Now, she was in her early thirties, and I was forty-five. That's a lot closer.

I can't tell you exactly when it happened. Things didn't change from one day to the next. It unfolded more organically, like a flower blooming. All I know is that I started thinking about her and looking forward to her visits more than I used to. Our letters caught this change and turned romantic, so gradually at first that I wondered if I was imagining it, and then later more rapidly. Then she started visiting more often.

We sat across from each other in the crowded cafeteria, eating hamburgers from the vending machine as other families visited with each other all around us. Contact with visitors was limited, but I couldn't stop myself from reaching out and touching her hair. At her next visit, I took her hand. It was maybe a week or two after that when I kissed her for the first time in that prison cafeteria.

I was starting to develop real feelings for Wendy, but the idea of starting a relationship was ridiculous with so much time left on my sentence. I hardly expected her to sit around like a wife waiting for her husband to return from war. Her life would move on over the next months and years while I was stuck inside. This was the very heartbreak of prison. That night, I wrote her a letter with a title: "The top ten reasons the kiss didn't mean anything." But as much as I resisted the idea that we had a chance, we both found ourselves believing that we did.

In so many ways, ours was an old-fashioned courtship. And I hate to say it, but it never would have been possible if I hadn't been in prison. At home, I was far too distracted, ping-ponging from one thought and one action to the next. It's not like my ADHD magically went away when I was inside, but with a lot less to do and far fewer distractions, it was easier for me to focus, to sit and actually finish a letter, which I never could have done back home. When Wendy visited, I had no choice but to fully listen and really see her, maybe for the first time. This made me a better person, and I liked the guy I was when we were together.

My visits with Wendy became my bright spots in an otherwise bleak existence. My work assignment at Coleman had been stacking books in the prison library, but I was messing around too much and got fired. I waited for my new assignment, and when it came, it was a nontraditional request. The guards asked if I would teach a business class to the other guys and offer them some tools to help them get work when they were eventually released. I was more than happy to do this, though I wasn't sure if the guys would be interested in what I had to say. We arranged for me to teach a couple nights a week in the rec room, so while the other guys were working, I had my days to work out in the rec yard, write letters to Wendy, read, and lie in my bunk, dreaming about being free.

On the night of my first class, I walked into the rec room expecting to find a few guys in folding chairs. Instead, the entire room was full. The seats were all taken and guys were standing along the cement walls waiting for me to begin. I'm not telling you this to say how great I am. The point is that there are far too few educational opportunities for prisoners. I wasn't even sure how much my little class could teach them, but these guys were hungry for any information they might be able to use when they were released.

I provided as much as I could, emphasizing that most of these guys probably already had the skills they needed to succeed. Just like at Eglin, most of the guys at Coleman had been locked up for selling drugs. "You were probably very successful selling crack or whatever," I told them. "So, take that entrepreneurial skill and put it toward something legal!"

That got a few laughs, but I meant every word of it. These guys were smart, and they clearly knew how to hustle. The differences between them and me were negligible. I had mostly just had better opportunities, but we had still all ended up in the same place. So as much as I taught them about profit margins, marketing, management techniques, and so on, I tried to instill the confidence that they could actually do this. I absolutely believed that, if given the chance, they could.

I loved teaching that class and connecting with the other guys, and it gave me a healthy outlet for my own energy and passion for entrepreneurship. Maybe that's why I was feeling so benevolent when my brother John came to visit and said that he needed a job. He was still working in the stock market, and I didn't know any details, but it seemed that his opportunities had dried up. Or maybe after seeing what had happened to me, he was worried about getting in trouble too.

A few years earlier, in the midst of my indictment and sentencing, John's drinking had hit a new low, and his kids had held an intervention for him. Since then, John had mostly stayed sober, and I could tell sitting across the table from him that he was sober now. I wanted to help him, but I wasn't sure what sort of role we could give him at the company. Now that he was sober again, he was somewhat back to his old, charming self, so I knew he could succeed in a client-facing role. But he had no experience in fashion or retail.

I had plenty of time to think it over as I lay in my bunk. Then one day it hit me. For years, we'd been talking about launching an international business, but it was a huge undertaking, and we were so busy expanding within the United States that we hadn't made it a priority. But John was all about rainmaking. He could charm clients and sell our shoes around the world, so I made him the head of international sales. I figured this was a low-risk move. Since we had no international sales yet to speak of, he couldn't mess it up.

John far from messed it up, though. He did an amazing job, even with a slow start in just a few countries. The first year we went global, our sales increased exponentially. It was hard for me to not be playing an active role in this chapter of the company's life, but knowing that my team was pulling through helped me stay positive as month after month ticked by.

Then, when I'd been at Coleman for almost an entire year, I was finally let into the drug and alcohol program. Just like that. Since it was a nine-month program, it wouldn't shave much time off of my sentence at that point. Come to think of it, maybe that's why they finally let me in. But I would have gladly done it if it meant getting released even one day sooner.

In the end, that five-hundred-dollar check to Belly's account cost me fourteen extra months in lockup. Unbelievable. But now that was all behind me. I finally had a release date—April 2005—and this gave me the strength to push on. Of course, having Wendy on my side, visiting more frequently and writing letters each day, helped too. A few months after our first kiss, our romance had snowballed. Her letters about how much she missed me and all the things we could do together after my release helped each day go by a little bit faster. And I found myself fantasizing about building a home with her and even starting a family.

During her next visit, we sat across from each other, holding hands over the table as Wendy told me a funny story about something that had happened at work. I was hardly listening. But for once I couldn't blame it on my ADHD. There was something on my mind that I had to say, and I was nervous.

"Steve, what is it?" Wendy asked, noticing how agitated I was.

I looked around the cafeteria. It wasn't the most romantic place for a proposal. Families sat just a few feet away from us, eating potato chips and talking. Some of them argued. Others embraced. I took a breath and stuttered out a few words about wanting to spend the rest of my life with her. Then I stopped myself, realizing that I wasn't making any sense. "What I'm trying to ask," I told her finally, "is if you'll marry me."

Wendy looked terrified. Or maybe she was shocked. But slowly a big smile started to spread across her face, and she nodded rapidly, wiping away tears. We both stood up, and I walked around to her side of the table for a kiss. The families around us looked over, sensing that something was going on. "We're getting married," I said to the small crowd, who all clapped and cheered as I grabbed hold of Wendy for another kiss.

It sounds made up, doesn't it? Like something out of a movie. But I swear that's how it went down. Even now, after all that's happened, I often think back to this moment and feel grateful for everything that led up to it—every day I spent in prison and even getting transferred to Coleman.

If it hadn't all happened exactly the way it did, who knows how different things might have been?

I don't know about the whole idea that everything happens for a reason. Sometimes I believe that, and then I see bad things happening to good people, and I have a hard time thinking it's really true. But as far as my life is concerned, I wouldn't change a thing. I screwed up, I paid my price, and I guess I had to go down that road to get to where I am now. But as I embraced Wendy in the cafeteria that day with so much to look forward to, I had no idea how amazing, and yet imperfect, my second act would be.

10
UPPER

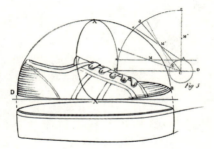

upper • the entire part of the shoe that covers the foot.

When the day finally came, I walked out of the Coleman Federal Correctional facility, got into Wendy's car, and we drove away. *Boom*. My time in prison was behind me, and life would never be the same.

Those first few days were a blur. We went out for sushi (hold the mackerel) and then got on a plane headed for New York. We were flying Jet Blue, and I flipped through the channels on the tiny screen on the seat back in front of me, amazed at how much had changed.

Altogether, I had been away for thirty-one months, a little more than two and a half years. In that time, the world had moved on. YouTube was born, fans had gone from being obsessed with pop stars to discovering unknown talents on shows like *American Idol*, and fashion trends had shifted from casual and grungy to more designer and label focused. I felt like Rip Van Winkle, who took a nap and woke up many years later. I had been alive and awake the whole time, but totally cut off from this cultural evolution.

Despite feeling anxious about all the changes coming at me, I was eager to dive back in to work and life, full of energy and determined not to squander my freedom. I knew that I had an opportunity to redeem myself and put the pieces of my life back together, and that I'd better not blow it. Maybe it would have been different if I'd been a lawyer or a stockbroker, but people in the fashion industry are pretty forgiving. I hoped they'd be willing to give me a second chance. At the same time, I knew I had to earn their forgiveness. And this time around, there were no shortcuts. To get my life back, I had to roll up my sleeves and dig in. I couldn't wait.

A lot of guys suffer from post-traumatic stress after spending time in prison, and I understand why. It's an awful, heartbreaking experience, and getting out is a painful reminder of all that you've missed. Plus, most guys don't have a fiancée and a company waiting for them when they're released, so it can be a huge challenge to adapt to life on the outside. I was lucky in so many ways. Instead of feeling traumatized, I was joyful, buoyant. There was so much coming at me, and I soaked it all in, feeling in some ways like a kid again seeing the world with fresh eyes. Everything I experienced felt brand new, from eating a slice of pizza to putting on a clean T-shirt. I hoped this feeling would last.

After a relaxing weekend with Wendy, I was desperate to get back to the office. First, I had to check into the halfway house in the Bronx where I'd be staying for the next two weeks. I was only allowed to leave the halfway house to go to work, and I had to be back by six o'clock each evening. I wasted no time and got to the office on my first day long before nine o'clock. I expected to be the first one there, but as I approached the familiar office building, I saw the entire team gathered around the front door, waiting to welcome me back. They clapped and cheered, "Welcome home, Steve!"

Indeed, this was home. It was all I could do to keep my emotions at bay. Shaking my head in disbelief, I went around to greet each person, one by one. I'd seen many of them throughout my time in prison during visitation, but others I hadn't laid eyes on in two and a half years. They noticed the physical changes that had taken place gradually while I was away.

"Look at you," Amelia said, giving me a hug. "You're such a tough guy." I reached up to remove my hat. In prison, I had replaced my baseball caps with knit beanies like the other guys wore.

"You like the old cue ball?" I asked.

"Yeah, and look at that muscle," Jamie said, punching me in the shoulder. "Looking good, man."

After a few minutes, we all went inside, and I headed straight to my office. It was such a comfort to be in there, with the picture of my high school golf team on the wall in front of me right next to a framed image of the Marilyn. I rubbed my palms together a few times before I sat down and said to no one in particular, "Alright, let's do this!"

On my desk sat printouts of a few ads the marketing team had run in anticipation of my return. I flipped through them one by one. The first showed one of our beautiful big-head girls wearing a pair of our high-platformed Slinkies and an ankle bracelet. The second featured a pair of sneakers above the words, "There's one pair of shoes that's been impossible to fill. Steve returns Spring 2005." And the third, which was running this week, simply read, "He's Back."

I smiled to myself. I knew this was the team's way of making light of my prison sentence while sending a signal to our customers and to Wall Street that we were confident about the company's future. The truth is that Wall Street probably needed to hear this message more than our customers themselves. Even with my indictment and prison sentence all over the news, most of the women who wore our shoes barely even knew there was a real guy named Steve Madden, never mind the fact that he had been to prison.

This was in large part thanks to the decision I had made back when I started the company to never put myself in our ads or make myself the face of the brand. At the time, I simply wanted the shoes to speak for themselves and figured that young women wouldn't have any interest in looking at my ugly mug. But now I realized that this had also saved the company from being punished for my personal mistakes.

Even these ads that referenced my time away still focused first and foremost on the real face of Steve Madden: our products. And that's what my team had been concentrating on in my absence too. Instead of trying to replace me as design chief while I was away, the team had built onto my vision by expanding into new retail and product areas. After years of planning, we finally launched our new STEVEN line, which moved us into a more grown-up market, and we'd licensed Candie's and Unionbay footwear for men to branch out further. Our retail business was strong. There were plans in the works to open fifteen new retail locations by the end of 2005, which would take us to a hundred stores in the United States.

On that first day and for the next several weeks, I met with as many people as I could to reacquaint myself with the team and every aspect of the business before making any big decisions. I wanted to take a moment and hear every detail of what had worked and what hadn't so we could figure out what was next. The team had done well overall, but some of them said they'd been running into each other without a leader. There had been too many committee meetings with no one there to make the hard choices and take risks when necessary.

I was raring to go and eager to be that person. But when the design team came to ask my opinion on the new shoe lines, I felt less confident. To some extent, business decisions can be made in a vacuum. A good business decision is a good business decision. But design is all about context. A shoe that's a hit now wouldn't have been a hit two years ago and won't be a hit two years from now either.

While I was away, there was a shift happening in fashion, as there is over any length of time. Young women were wearing fancier, more high-end shoes instead of the chunky platforms our brand was known for. The team had responded by making dressier, less quirky shoes. But they had no choice but to price those shoes a little higher, and this turned off some of our core customers.

To figure out a solution, Rachelle, Karla, Rob, and I held tons of product meetings in my office. There was always an additional smattering of folks sitting on the couch or on the floor so I could solicit their opinions too. Those meetings lasted for hours as we tried to create our next hit or, we hoped, a full line of hits.

After just a few days, I began to get a sense of the trends, and ideas started pouring in. With samples surrounding me, I grabbed a ballet flat with ribbons. "This is great," I said, but my mind was elsewhere. I could have sworn I'd seen a sample of a pump with shiny silver heels. It was sexy, and our "Steve Madden girls" would love it. But I couldn't find it anywhere in the piles of shoes on my desk, the couch, or the floor.

"I like the idea of having some shoes with metal heels," I said. "Maybe this is the right time for those." Wandering from pile to pile, I rifled through the samples until I came across a multi-strap shoe that I thought would work with the metal heels. "This is gonna be a hot shoe," I told the team. "Hot. Take this upper, put it on the metal heels, you're done with it. That's the shoe. Let's sell the shit out of it."

They took the shoes to the sample factory, and within an hour they were back with two shoes: one in shiny metallic leather with a silver heel and one in black patent leather with a chrome heel. I turned them over in my hands. "Would you wear the silver?" I asked Karla.

My team didn't just help me design, produce, market, and merchandise my shoes. They were my full-time focus group. Some of the women who worked for me had a downtown, grungy aesthetic. Others were Roosevelt Field girls. I knew which shoes would work in each market and solicited opinions accordingly. Feeling out of touch with the trends after being away, I relied on my team more than ever.

The best team members, like Karla, were the ones I knew would be honest with me instead of just saying that everything was great. If she said that she would wear a shoe, there was a good chance it was going to be a hit. She nodded thoughtfully. "Definitely. The black might be too much with the chrome, but the silver is cool."

Rob agreed. "That is what girls like to wear."

"Let's do it," I said, and they went off again to have a dozen pairs of the silver pump made and placed in the SoHo store by noon.

Every day went like this. One minute, I'd look at the clock and it was ten, and then the next thing I knew it was five o'clock, and I had to rush back to the halfway house. It was the greatest feeling, an incredible high to be back on this team inspiring others and being inspired by them too.

I had just barely gotten back in the swing of things, but I was eager to reinvigorate the company by making some new hires. While I was in prison, I had gotten a letter from a young guy named Ed Rosenfeld who worked at PJ SOLOMON, a financial services company that had done some work for us while I was away. Ed's letter explained that he wanted to get out of banking and work at a company where he could learn a business and make decisions and then live with them. He wrote that with his finance background, he believed he could help bring our company to the next level.

I liked the sound of that, and called Ed to ask him to come in and meet with me. "I'm in Mexico this week," Ed told me. "I can come in any day next week."

I shook my head, as if he could hear that over the phone. "No," I told him. "If you want to meet, be here tomorrow." I hung up. I don't know why I had an urge to test Ed so soon. I guess I wanted to see how serious he was about working with me. Of course I would have met with him the following week, but I didn't have to because he showed up in my office the next day.

Ed has been one of the most important hires in the history of Steve Madden, so I want to break down the traits I recognized in him that day. First, he had an instinct to be a maker, which I admired. And beyond being sharp, which he clearly was, Ed was as cool and dispassionate as I was excitable and over-the-top. We had complementary skills, but, like me, Ed was clearly an entrepreneur.

To me, being an entrepreneur doesn't have to mean starting a business. It can be anyone who breaks the rulebook and has a creative way of doing things. Not everyone I hire is an entrepreneur. It takes all kinds of people to make the business go. Some of my best team members excel at blocking and tackling, meaning they are solid executives who just know how to get shit done. They may not get the glory, but we couldn't thrive as a company without them.

Ed, however, was an entrepreneur, and in addition, he had the one trait that I consider most important in an executive, and that is the ability to think small and think big at the same time. To succeed in our business, we do both every day. We have to obsess over the tiniest details, like getting a case of shoes delivered to a store by Friday. But at the same time, we need to always have our eyes on the big picture—where the company is going in the next eighteen months, what next year's shoe line will look like, and what positions we need to fill. I sensed right away that Ed had this skill.

On top of that, Ed was emotionally healthy. This may seem like a crazy thing to screen for when hiring, but it's so important for executives not to get caught up in their own egos. I have always thought that I'm a bit of an egomaniac or even a narcissist. At the heart of every addict lies a narcissist. We're so obsessed with ourselves and our own experiences that it's overwhelming, and booze and drugs seem like the only possible escapes.

Since I've been in recovery, I've been fighting my ego, and I've developed rituals to help me resist my narcissistic tendencies. When I sit down with someone, I force myself to ask the other person questions instead of just talking about myself. Of course, all I want to do is talk about myself. And I constantly check my ego at work. The most successful meetings are the ones where a big decision is made and five different people leave the room each thinking it was their idea. When you're driven by ego, your impulse is to make sure everyone knows it was your idea. But at the end of the day, there's no scoreboard. The company wins when the team has ownership.

Another way the ego gets in the way at work is when someone receives a piece of information, like which shoe is a best seller right now. Most people will respond from the ego by saying, "I knew that already." But an emotionally healthy person doesn't need to tell the other person that he or she is in the know. Someone like Ed would simply thank the other person for the information. As an egomaniac myself, I get so mad when I see other people doing the same ego-driven things I do, and once I calm down that's how I learn not to do them anymore.

With all these traits, I knew I wanted Ed on the team, despite the fact that I didn't really have a role in mind for him. "Just come in and we'll figure it out," I told him. We made up a title, something to do with strategic planning, but it was just an excuse to get him on the team.

I figured that if Ed was going to learn the business, he might as well learn it directly from me. So, at first Ed worked right out of my office. He sat on the couch next to my desk with his laptop propped on the coffee table and participated in every meeting and conversation I had, whether it was about marketing, finances, or, most often, products. During our brief moments of down time, I told him stories from my time in prison and played him the rap music that Swole, Tuna, Neville, and the other guys had taught me to love.

After two weeks, I could finally move out of the halfway house and experience complete freedom. Wendy had rented a townhouse for us on the Upper East Side and had it all set up with pink and purple furniture and sparkly objects everywhere. I found a new meeting to attend nearby and went every day when I wasn't traveling. Some of my friends thought I was nuts to move right in with Wendy and immediately start planning a wedding, but we were excited to move our relationship forward, and it was incredibly helpful to have Wendy on my side as I continued to find my footing.

With no more curfew or constraints on my time, I got back to my old tricks, pounding the pavement with my eyes on women's feet. As soon as I got out on the street and into our stores, I pulled together the shoes my team had been working on and added new styles to create a complete line that included some massive hits.

As our shoes had gotten fancier to keep up with the trends, they had lost some of their edge, so we worked hard to put that back in while staying current. Ballet flats, like the ones I'd seen with the ribbons, were big that year, so we added buckles and jewels to make ours more playful. Then we added a four-inch peep toe pump with bold stripes and a bow across the toe, and suede fringed heels to capitalize on the BoHo chic look that was hot at the moment.

More than ever, our ability to quickly produce these shoes and put them right in the store proved invaluable. I sat in our SoHo store with Karla during one of my first weekends back and, feeling hugely energized and relieved, watched as women snapped up shoes from the new line. I hadn't let on to my team, but when I first got out, I wasn't sure that I could recapture the old magic. I knew the company itself was solid. In many ways, it was even better off than it had been before I went away, because my team had stepped up and stopped relying so much on me. But in our business, product is king.

While I'm a hard-nosed worrier who's always been conservative with the business, in order to succeed you have to be willing to try new things. Without a strong leader dictating when to take a risk and when to play it safe, the company hadn't exactly gone downhill, but it had gone sideways. And I was so grateful now to be able to provide the shot in the arm that we needed to move forward.

I had always been relentless, but now I had the extra boost of feeling like a survivor. There was some esteem built from being able to survive the awful prison conditions and, frankly, even flourish in that environment. I poured that spirit into the company when it needed it most.

Before the year was out, we had made a huge comeback. The stock had tripled and our sales rose to five hundred million dollars. We weren't the same company we had been before I'd gone to prison, but we were so much better in so many ways.

It was an equally exciting time for me personally, though that high wouldn't last as long as the company's explosive growth. In January of 2006, just nine months after I was released from prison, Wendy and I got married. My instinct was to go to Vegas and do it quietly, but it didn't turn out that way. Instead, our wedding was a big affair at the Rainbow Room on top of 30 Rockefeller Plaza in Manhattan.

It was a beautiful wedding, and I was glad that my mom and brothers could be there. I don't think they ever expected to see me get married. And, to be honest, I never really did, either. My whole life, I'd always felt like an outcast. I was a creature of the night, an addict, someone who did things differently and never even tried to fit the mold. It wasn't that I didn't *want* to be normal. I just wasn't made that way. And while I'd learned to embrace my differences and make the most of them, it still didn't feel entirely natural to be doing something as ordinary as getting married, especially at this big, traditional wedding with a huge white cake and a live band.

So, as happy as I was that day, and I was very happy, I also felt like I was out of my element: itchy in my tux, out of tune with the formality of it all. Wendy was normal, and I mean that in the nicest possible way. She was wholesome and well liked and knew how to take care of herself. When people heard we were engaged, those who knew us both said in shock, "She's marrying *him*?" They couldn't believe it. And sometimes I couldn't either. I worried that I was too weird for her, and found myself doing things, like agreeing to this wedding, to prove that I wasn't really rogue. But then I'd retreat into my uniqueness as a form of protection, like a turtle hiding in its shell.

At first, I liked the normalcy of being married—having a partner to do things with and to take care of me—and we wanted to start a family right away. We knew the math wasn't on our side, so we started trying in earnest immediately. It was a lot of pressure to keep track of the timing and focus on having children instead of making love. I'm not the first person to note that this puts a strain on a marriage, and of course it was much harder on Wendy than it was for me. And, anyway, it wasn't working. After trying for about a year, we decided to do in vitro. It took right away, and Wendy became pregnant with twins. We were thrilled.

It was around this time that I got a couple calls I'd been hoping to receive ever since I was transferred out of Eglin. My assistant came into my office one morning with a confused look on her face. "There's someone on the phone for you," she told me. "He says his name is Swole?"

I pounced on the phone. "My man, what's happening?"

"Yo, shoe man, you never got me those boots I was looking for." It was so great to hear Swole's voice completely out of context. "I just got out, and my girl's pissed at me, man. She's saying I don't really know you."

I laughed into the phone. "We'll get you some shoes. Don't worry, man," I told him. "But what else do you need? Do you have a job? Do you want to do something?"

Swole was still down in Florida, so I got him a job working with Luke in our warehouse down there. Not long after, Neville reached out after he was released. He was living in Louisiana, and we gave him a job working in one of our stores. Over time, four or five other guys I'd done time with reached out, and we found them work at the company too.

People acted like I was doing this remarkable thing by hiring these guys, but they were great employees and hard workers. It was a no-brainer to hire them. Sure, they had messed up in the past, but they still deserved opportunities. I had screwed up, too, and I'd had my second chance handed to me, no questions asked. I was grateful that my advantages allowed me to give those guys a second chance too.

I don't know if he heard that I was hiring these guys from prison or not, but around this time another old friend reached out. Bradley and I had worked together at Toulouse way back in high school. We hadn't really kept in touch, but I saw him once in a while in the old neighborhood and later around the city. He wanted to introduce me to a local nonprofit organization that helped men who were formerly homeless, incarcerated, and/or struggling with addiction find work, housing, educational opportunities, counseling, and career training.

Bradley came into the office to meet with Wendy and me, and the two of them hit it off right away. I was happy to reconnect with Bradley, but I didn't need him to sell me on getting involved. I had seen firsthand how the cycle of incarceration, addiction, and unemployment destroyed so many lives, especially in the black community, and I was eager to do what I could to help. Wendy and I went to talk to the guys and offer our support, volunteered, and hired as many of them as possible.

It always felt like I wasn't doing enough. I've gotten involved in several organizations over the years, but the incarceration issue in this country is so huge that it doesn't make a dent. I guess if you can help one guy, it's a lot. I have to look at it that way. But knowing the reality of prison, it's tough not to think about all the guys I can't help, instead of the relative few I can.

People often asked me how I felt after getting out of prison, if I had survivor's guilt or a new sense of purpose or what. More than anything, I just felt lucky. So many fortuitous things happened along my journey. Looking back at how the ball bounced, I got some pretty good bounces. Of course, I got some bad bounces, too, but even those led me to the right place in the end.

It was hard to believe where I was, in a beautiful apartment with a gorgeous wife and two kids on the way. I couldn't explain how all that had happened, but I knew that a lot of it came down to luck. And helping other guys when I could was just my way of thanking the universe.

During this time, Wendy and I had gotten to know Bradley and his partner, David, who were both involved in multiple charitable organizations. They were such decent guys, and we loved spending time with them. One day, Wendy asked me what I thought about asking the two of them to act as godfathers for the twins. We knew we would be raising our kids with an enormous amount of privilege, and Wendy wanted to find ways to offset this by giving them some perspective and teaching them how important it was to give back. Bradley and David agreed right away, and as our relationship deepened, they continued to help me find new ways to give back too.

Don't get me wrong. I was the same selfish egomaniac as always, especially when it came to work. By then, we no longer held shoe shows at the Plaza Hotel. Instead, we had our own showroom in Manhattan, a massive maze-like sprawl of rooms holding the new season's styles for each of our lines. I was in the Steve Madden showroom one day with Danny Friedman, whose handbags, belts, and small leather goods we licensed for the Steve Madden brands. This accessories line had been doing well, and I felt ownership of Danny's company, DMF Accessories, but I didn't actually own it.

When a stream of people started coming into the showroom to look at the handbags, I started to get suspicious that Danny was trying to sell his company. He had every right to do that, of course, but I didn't like it. I thought of them as ours. So, I marched to the back of the showroom and made an offer to buy the company outright. Ed helped me put together the deal, and within a month, we owned DMF Accessories.

This acquisition, borne out of my own jealousy, marked the beginning of a new chapter for Steve Madden. Though we had been branching out over the years, we were still primarily known for making shoes for teenagers. Most of the time, bigger companies eventually acquire brands like ours. Instead, we became the ones that acquired other companies while growing into new markets, and this launched the company to a new level.

Before prison, my entire life was singularly focused on my obsessive drive to "make it." Now I was even more determined to succeed than ever, with my sense of redemption wrapped up in each deal and every shoe.

But in the fall of 2007, there was finally something in my life that came before the business: a little boy named Jack and a girl named Stevie.

In some ways, fatherhood was an even bigger shock to my system than prison had been. Everything about being a parent was so counter-intuitive, especially for a selfish guy like me. I simply couldn't be selfish around my kids. It had to be all about them. I accepted this and even relished it because I saw that it was forcing me to become a better person, even if it was against my will.

Wendy, on the other hand, took to motherhood right away. Of course, she had plenty of help, so she was able to enjoy her time with the twins, and she had fun with it. Jack and Stevie weren't identical, obviously, but they did look a lot alike as babies, with my strawberry blond hair and Wendy's striking eyes. Whenever friends came over, she'd dress them in each other's clothes just to see if they could tell the difference. Bradley and David were the only ones who ever could. As soon as the twins could walk, Wendy would chase them around the house and tickle them. I'd come home from work to find the three of them cuddled up together taking a nap or giggling in a heap after a tickle fight.

But I don't think anyone was as happy for me to become a father as the people on my team. For years, I'd been looking at them sideways when they said they had to go to their kids' dance recital or soccer game, but I finally understood how it felt to want to be somewhere other than the office or a shoe store.

Having kids also gave me something new to worry about, and, as crazy as it sounds, this helped me focus at work. We have a corporate ethos at Steve Madden, and that is: We're panickers. We panic a lot. From the moment I started the company, I thought we were going out of business, and I drilled this sense of caution and doom into my team the same way my dad had drilled it into me. And I now had a whole team of people who were as passionate and panicked and full of creative ambition as I was. The twins' birth coincided with a period of enormous growth for the company. Rest was over, and there was a new energy at the company that gave us the wind at our back.

The time had come for a change and, like most changes, I knew this one wasn't going to be easy. Part of my sentence had been a seven-year ban from acting as an officer or executive of the company, and those seven years were almost up. Many people assumed that I would just go back to being CEO as soon as I could, but now that I had seen how useful it was to have someone else in that role, I had no interest in doing that.

This is one of many reasons I'm so grateful for every step of my journey, including the most painful ones. If I hadn't gone away, I probably would have stayed on as CEO indefinitely, and I'm certain that if I had, we wouldn't be nearly as successful a company as we are today. After being forced to step aside, I saw that my talent was not to be the CEO of Steve Madden. I *am* Steve Madden. The CEO has to take calls all day and deal with confrontation and stay organized and, worst of all, remain calm. Impossible! The truth is I wasn't suited to it.

I was aware of my limitations, but I also knew that I had certain talents. Putting the pieces together was one thing, but my focus was mostly on choosing the right people and energizing the team like an effective coach. While those guys don't play in the game, they do something indescribable that helps the team win. The same is true for me, and I saw this more clearly than ever after returning from prison. Why did our profits increase so much after I got out? It wasn't due to any specific thing I did. It was just about picking the right people and finding ways to motivate them to do great things.

After spending so much time with Ed and seeing how instrumental he was to the deals we'd been making, not to mention the traits I saw in him that first day, I knew he was the right choice to be our new CEO. Ed was unbelievably smart, and he understood the ramifications of every detail of a deal. I wanted him leading the charge as the company moved forward, and luckily the board of directors agreed.

Jamie had taken over as CEO when I was at my lowest point and afraid of losing everything, and he had done exactly what I had needed him to do while I was away. He was a good listener who took care of the team, and he did a fantastic job of maintaining stability and keeping things in line. I was so grateful to him, and I'm positive the company would not still be here if it weren't for Jamie's thoughtful leadership during his tenure. But now I was back. We no longer needed someone filling in for me. Instead, we needed someone who could complement me to take the company to the next level, one I could still barely even envision.

I'd known Jamie since we were kids, and it was difficult asking him to step down. We offered him a generous severance package for a job well done, and I hoped we would stay friends. And then, to the shock of Wall Street and everyone in the fashion industry, I hired Ed, a thirty-two-year-old kid, to be the CEO of Steve Madden. He proved himself right away, expertly making two major licensing deals for us within his first year. One was with Kimora Lee Simmons to distribute her line of footwear and accessories in J. C. Penney, and the other was to distribute the L.e.i. franchise at Wal-Mart.

These deals were just the beginning. While our pre-prison success was creatively groundbreaking and established a large footprint for us as a company, with Ed as CEO, our company's business acumen caught up with our brand's creative power. And with that package together, we were unstoppable.

11
GENTLEMAN'S CORNER

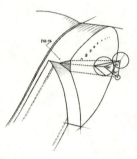

gentleman's corner • developed in the 1930s, this involved slicing
off the instep of the corner of the heel to prevent men's
trouser hems from catching on their shoes.

was sitting on the toilet, an exceptionally fitting place, reading *The Wolf of Wall Street*. Jordan and I hadn't seen each other since our court battle many years earlier. While I didn't hold a grudge against him, I was curious to see what he had to say in his book. I was reading a chapter devoted to me, which was aptly called "The Cobbler." That nickname is really the only thing from our time together that has stuck. Jordan was always big on nicknames, but he just went by Jordan or sometimes JB. No one ever called him "The Wolf of Wall Street." It's a great title, but I had never heard of that name until I found out he was writing a book.

Only eighty-something pages in, Jordan had already called me "one of the least fashionable dressers on the planet" and "an over-the-top artsy-fartsy guy." Worst of all, he called the Mary Lou "a horrendous-looking platform shoe." I didn't take offense, but at the same time, I asked myself what the hell I was doing. Why was I reading this, just to get myself upset? I threw the book in the garbage and went about my day, hoping (unrealistically) that this would be the first and last time I ever heard of *The Wolf of Wall Street*.

Things were going so well, and I wasn't going to let any book get in the way. Jack and Stevie were toddlers now and thriving, and so was the business. That year, we launched Madden Music, a cobranding venture with different musical artists who performed at our stores and helped promote the brand. I always thought that the music business was parallel to the shoe business. There's a reason you see so many music icons creating their own fashion lines. Music inspires fashion and vice versa, and music has always been a central part of my inspiration, whether it was the glam rock from my early years, the grunge music of the 1990s that informed my early styles, or the country music I still have an affinity for. But it was pop music that most often shaped the trends in fashion, so these were the artists we wanted to partner with on this new venture.

Our goal was to support the emerging artists who would resonate with our core customers: the young, fashionable girls who loved our shoes. Marketing was now a vastly different terrain compared to when I had started the business. Back then, we simply made a hot shoe and sold it to stores. Then we started running ads. Now it wasn't enough to create a great product and even to advertise it. We had to constantly find new ways to get our brand name out there and make sure it was synonymous with being cool. Partnering with celebrities was the most effective and efficient way to do this.

Thankfully, I had a top-notch marketing team who could pair our old-school approach to business with the exciting new marketing ventures. They were constantly coming up with new ideas. Or maybe they just left the meeting thinking it was their idea. Madden Music was one of many.

Katy Perry's first album had just been released, and "I Kissed a Girl" was at the top of the charts. At the time, she was rocking a retro, pinup vibe that was a good match for our shoes. The same young women who loved Steve Madden listened to her music. We hosted a live performance at our store on the Lower East Side of Manhattan and then aired it in all our stores around the country.

Soon after, Gabriella Weiser, our vice president of marketing, came to me with another idea. "I've got this artist who is about to explode," she told me. "I really like her." She played me a few songs from Lady Gaga's debut record, and I was sold.

It was so much fun working with Gaga, and afterward it was incredible to see her go on to become a global icon. She's continued to be a good friend to the company, too, wearing our shoes and even putting her backup dancers in our boots for her Super Bowl performance.

Over time, our music venture grew bigger and bigger and went from in-store performances to large concert venues and even a presence at festivals like Coachella. We also started branching out into partnerships with nonmusical celebrities. One of our first celebrity collaborations was with Mary-Kate and Ashley Olsen on shoes for their high-end Elizabeth and James fashion line.

When we announced this partnership, people in the fashion industry were horrified. They didn't understand how a company like Steve Madden, which was known for making shoes for teenagers, could create high-fashion shoes for Elizabeth and James's sophisticated, older customers. This is the exact sort of narrow-minded thinking I have been fighting against my whole career. Making a high-end product is no more difficult than making something affordable. At a higher price point, you simply have more flexibility in what materials you can use. You can take more liberties. But at the end of the day, it's the same process. Mary-Kate and Ashley knew what they wanted, and we worked hard to create shoes together that fit their vision and were embraced by their fans.

At one of our meetings, I noticed that Ashley was wearing an old, beat-up pair of white sneakers. I recognized them right away as Supergas, casual, rubber-soled sneakers that Italians had been wearing for generations but were almost completely unknown in the States. They're sort of like the Italian version of Keds. Ever since I had started scouting in Europe in the 1980s, they had been my favorite sneakers. I was impressed that Ashley had even heard of them.

"Those are great," I told her, lightly kicking her foot with the toe of my penny loafer. "I've always wanted to buy that company."

Ashley brightened immediately. "Well, if you do, please think of us," she said. "We'd love to be involved in some way."

A couple years later, we signed a deal with Superga to become its exclusive licensee in the United States, and I hired Mary-Kate and Ashley to be our creative directors. While the trendy styles that Steve Madden is known for are constantly evolving, Superga's style was classic. We had no intention of changing that. Our goal was to bring awareness of the brand to the market. Mary-Kate and Ashley had another clothing line by then, The Row. They created a capsule collection of luxury Supergas for The Row and worked on creating marketing and distribution opportunities for the classic Supergas.

As we expanded, a big part of our strategy was also to partner with and acquire companies that would help us grow into new areas. *Footwear News* named us Company of the Year in 2009, and one reason we were so successful was that we owned such a large share of the market. We had the Steve Madden brand at Nordstrom, the Elizabeth and James line at Neiman Marcus, and L.e.i. at Wal-Mart. As a result, we had more hits at one time, but fewer of those big number-one hits that everyone knew by name like the Marilyn or the Slinky. Our top sellers still sold just as much as those iconic shoes did in their heydays, but we had ten other shoes selling maybe 70 percent as much at the same time.

Ed was the architect of these deals, and he put them together masterfully. People talk about how my platform shoes changed the fashion industry. I was one of the first designers to market directly to teen girls, to democratize trends, and to focus on speed to market. But the way Ed has used our capital to purchase other companies and branch out into more and more areas in the market has been just as revolutionary. Finding Ed was a lucky break. I can't take credit for it beyond recognizing his talent when he walked into my office, but I'm grateful every day that I did.

By 2010, our new accessories line, DMF, had proven to be a home run. We knew we wanted to do more in that space, so we purchased Zone 88, a company that designed and marketed private label accessories for mass merchants and midtier retailers. The next year, I noticed at the shoe shows that a trendy handbag company called Big Buddha with great products always had a very busy booth, so we purchased it too.

That same year, we learned that Betsey Johnson's company had fallen into disrepair. They were bankrupt and had defaulted on a forty-eight-million-dollar loan. We already held the license for handbags, small leather goods, belts, and umbrellas under the Betsey Johnson and Betseyville trademarks, so it made sense for us to buy out the loan, effectively buying Betsey Johnson.

This was a smart business move, and personally I loved the idea of our brands uniting. I didn't know Betsey well, but of course we had crossed paths many times over the years, and I had always liked her. For a certain type of rebellious, fashionable girl who came of age in the 1990s, Betsey Johnson and Steve Madden were already inexorably linked. Now it was finally official.

When word got out that we were buying Betsey Johnson, some people worried that it was some sort of hostile takeover and we were trying to buy the brand out from under Betsey. The opposite was true. Of course, we're always looking to profit, but we also wanted to give Betsey's brand a second chance. We chose certain companies to acquire because we saw their potential and wanted to help offer a larger platform. We would never march in there and say, "We're the boss now; you do what I say!" That would undermine the success of the company. Part of the acquisition was always the talent behind the brand, and we valued that. Betsey Johnson was certainly no exception, and our partnership has proved very successful, for us and for them.

But nowhere were we expanding more rapidly than in our international business. My brother John had taken the opportunity to lead our international expansion and run with it, and our growth overseas was bigger and better than any of us had imagined. This was the most successful John had ever been in his life, and he came to it late. He was now about sixty years old, had been diagnosed with pulmonary disease (COPD), and often had trouble breathing. But his doctors said they caught it early, and fortunately he had plenty of time left.

Like all addicts, John still struggled, but he was sober most of the time, as was his wife, Sherri. They still lived in Florida, and John traveled back and forth to New York. Whenever they were in town, John and Sherri spent a lot of time with the twins and became their favorite uncle and auntie.

As I had hoped, this job proved to be a perfect fit for John's skills. He was an expert schmoozer, a great seller, and a big thinker—a much bigger thinker than me, actually. I can't make a simple decision without asking a hundred people for their opinions. When we were talking about whether to collaborate with Madonna on a line of shoes for Macy's, Ed teased me, "Do you want to ask the UPS guy what he thinks?" It had always been a part of my process to talk things over with everyone. But John just went and did it, approaching one country at a time and selling them on our brand.

John also understood the importance of entertaining clients. He was a genuinely kind guy, but he was also a showman. He took clients out to lavish dinners, bought them the most expensive bottles of champagne, flew them on the private jet, and ordered Dungeness crab for the flight. Meanwhile, I still agonized about how much lunch cost whenever we ordered in for a meeting.

When I saw John's expense bills, I nearly lost my mind. "What the fuck are you doing?" I asked him.

"What do you think I'm doing?" he asked me, dumbfounded by my shortsightedness. "I'm bringing you an entire country!"

"That's not how we do business," I told him.

"Look at how successful you are," he said. "Why are you so unhappy?"

But I wasn't unhappy. I was just stuck in my small ways, afraid as ever that the sky was about to fall.

Of course, John was right. By 2010, just five years after we launched our international business, we were selling shoes in forty-six countries and had eighty-one of our own stores overseas. John's strategy was to find strong local retailers who knew the shoe business and could help us open retail stores in the area. As we did in the United States, we prioritized pairing wholesale and retail business in each new country we entered.

It was especially gratifying for me to see that our styles successfully spanned the globe. Before we launched our international business, I worried that we wouldn't be able to predict trends in other cultures the way we could in the United States. After all, I couldn't park myself in a shoe store in every country and watch women buy shoes to see which way the winds of trends were blowing. But our top ten styles at any given time were virtually identical around the world. A cool shoe in New York was still a cool shoe in London, Tokyo, and Dubai. I loved to see that.

I was so happy for John's success, not only for selfish reasons but also because my big brother, whom I had always idolized, was finally living up to his potential. For so long, I had hoped to one day see the same thing for Luke, that he would get sober and have a wonderful life. But it didn't turn out that way. It's painful, but alcoholism is a disease, and that's just the way it is.

In 2008, Luke had a massive stroke that left him in a wheelchair and in need of around-the-clock care. I flew down to Florida to see Luke and help set up his care. When I talked to him, he seemed to know who I was, but the subjects morphed. It was very difficult. While I was in Florida, I also went to see my mom. She had been diagnosed with Alzheimer's a few years earlier and was still pretty cognizant for the most part, but there were times when her mind started to slip. I wasn't sure how much she understood about what had happened to Luke.

When I got to her house, she was sitting on the floral couch in her living room looking frail. A housekeeper was washing dishes in the sink. I approached my mom, trying to act like everything was normal. "What's up, Mama?" I asked in a loud voice as I crossed the living room toward her. She reached her fragile arms out to me, and I bent down to give her a gentle hug before sitting on the couch beside her.

My mom held onto both my hands and looked at me. For the past few years, I was never sure what to say to her. It was hard to tell how much she understood, but I did my best to entertain her with stories and pictures of Wendy and the twins. She loved that. But now it looked like she had something to say. "What's up, Mama?" I repeated, looking down at her.

She tightened her grip on my hands. "I was so wrong," she said, looking right into my eyes. "So wrong."

I silently pulled out my phone to show her some new pictures of the kids, but I knew what she was trying to say. My whole life, my mom had thought of me as the bad kid. And you know what? She was right. I *was* a bad kid. But even though I had made mistakes and even gone to prison, she recognized that I had turned out to be a good boy. I was the one taking care of my brothers and her and doing what I could to help other people.

On one hand, it was a big moment for me. I was redeemed for my past sins in my mother's eyes. What son doesn't want that? But on the other hand, it was too late. I knew who I was by then: a flawed man who had done some exceptional things. I owned this in full, despite what anyone said. But it was still nice to hear.

While I was in Florida, I also visited John's wife, Sherri, and their daughter, Kira, who was now in her teens. I had a good relationship with Shawn and Blake, John's sons from his first marriage, and I wanted to have the same kind of connection to Kira.

We had just designed a pump for Steve Madden that was close to a Louboutin, and this was before anyone even knew about Louboutins. Ours only cost a little over a hundred bucks, while the real Louboutins were somewhere around seven hundred. I walked into the house in Parkland, Florida, and the first thing I saw was a pair of Kira's red-soled Louboutins lying on the floor.

I was so upset. "What, do you think you're too good for Steve Maddens?" I tried to say it in a jovial tone, but it was obvious that I wasn't joking.

"I bought her those," Sherri responded. "Why shouldn't she have them?"

"She's a sixteen-year-old kid," I said. "What does she need seven-hundred-dollar shoes for? And the only reason you can afford to buy them for her is because her dad is making money at Steve Madden."

If Kira had been making her own money, that would have been one thing. She could wear whatever shoes she wanted. But the way I saw it, she was making a statement that she was above wearing the very shoes that were putting food in her mouth and, ironically, Louboutins on her feet. I couldn't stand for that.

Look, I'm not perfect. The writer Marge Piercy said, "My strengths and my weaknesses are twins in the same womb." My work ethic, my pride in my company, my impatience, and my passion had gotten me so far, but I couldn't turn them off when the moment called for it. It may seem completely draconian or even insane to get so angry about Kira wearing Louboutins instead of my shoes. I'm still walking around with this resentment today. Trust me—that hurts me more than it hurts anyone else. But these are the principles I live with.

And while we're on the subject, let's talk about whether we knocked off those Louboutins. During these years, several high-end fashion designers sued Steve Madden for allegedly ripping off their styles. We weren't alone. Every fashion house gets sued, especially those working at our price point.

Every shoe company is looking for inspiration in the same places: the market, the trends, and everything else that's out there in the zeitgeist. It's a big stew, a gumbo of popular styles, influences from overseas, unique designs, and so on. As we design our shoes, we're mixing that stew in our own particular way, adding our own spices, and it comes out as Steve Madden.

The expensive, high-end shoes that we allegedly knock off are certainly ingredients that we include in our stew. We try to capture their spirit and bring that to our "Steve Madden girls," almost like a variation of the same theme. We always try to add enough of our own flavor and seasonings so the resulting stew tastes uniquely like Steve Madden. Once in a while, it tastes too much like the stew from next door. I admit that. But it's never intentional.

All told, this is very infrequent. We create thousands and thousands of styles, but it only makes headlines once every few years when a high-end fashion house sues us for allegedly ripping them off. The truth is that we get copied far more than we're accused of copying other designers. There are knock-off Steve Madden shoes all over China, but that's not as interesting for the fashion industry to talk about.

That's OK. In 2011, we made a big move into China by buying Topline, a private label company out of Seattle. We wanted to boost our own private label business, and more important, Topline had the best sourcing base in northern China. By hitching our wagon to them, we were able to set up an infrastructure in China that included three offices and six hundred employees. Without having to go through agents, we could get better prices and higher margins for our products while retaining the same quality.

The same year, we purchased Cejon, an accessories company that had held our scarf and cold weather license since 2006. At that point, our accessories business was basically limited to handbags, small leather goods, and belts, so this acquisition offered us an opportunity to extend our reach into new areas of the market. *Footwear News* named us Company of the Year again in 2011.

All this growth required long hours and a tremendous amount of travel. I was on the road a lot, and when I was home, my mind was still on work. Wendy would try to tell me about something cute one of the twins had done, and I'd be half-listening while checking the stock price on my phone, texting Ed about a specific deal point, and thinking about which artist we might want to collaborate with next. *My strengths and weaknesses are twins in the same womb.* With the kids I could be present, or present enough. I loved playing with them, tossing them in the air, and being silly. But it wasn't easy for Wendy to get my full attention.

Wendy was incredibly supportive of the work and of golf, my greatest love outside of work. But she was still human. She often joked that she missed having me in prison, and it hurt to know that deep down she meant every word. Even worse, I knew she was right. I was a better guy when I was in prison. I had come out with a new sense of purpose, determined to reinvigorate the company and also to give back. With Bradley and David's help, I found new organizations to get involved in and donate to, and I continued to help people when I could and give jobs to those in need. But I was still me, and relationships weren't any easier for me to sustain. Somehow, I had been better able to adapt to life in prison than to married life.

Shoes covered every inch of our townhouse. They were scattered across the kitchen table, my nightstand, and covered the floor of every room. Whenever I was talking to Wendy, I was also holding one of our newest styles, turning it over in my hands, feeling the leather and trying to determine if it would be our next hit. When she got really annoyed with me, she put a pair of shoes right on my pillow to make a point, or perhaps to question where my loyalties really lay.

Slowly, distance began to grow between us, and that space allowed resentment to flourish. At the dinner table, I liked to say funny prayers and make faces to try to make the kids laugh. But every time I cracked a joke, Wendy would roll her eyes. So, I stopped doing it. Before long, I felt like I was walking on eggshells and couldn't be myself in the relationship.

I'm not blaming Wendy. I'm sure she harbored her own resentments, and they were likely justified. When I was on the road for work, I'd call home, and I started to dread those daily check-ins.

"What's doing?" I asked when Wendy picked up the phone.

"Not much." There was silence. At first, I thought she was going to speak again, but then there was nothing. I pulled the phone from my ear to look at the screen and see if we'd been disconnected.

"Are you there?"

"Yeah, I'm here." Then it was silence again.

It went on like this for a while, and then when the twins were almost five, Wendy got pregnant again. It was a complete surprise, unlike the first time, and she was thrilled. I was fifty-five and worried that I was too old to become a father again, but I was excited at the same time. I felt boxed in by the marriage, and by then Wendy and I had gone from walking on eggshells to fighting constantly, but I loved being with the kids. They were my raison d'être, my reason to live. One of the main reasons I had wanted to get married was to become a father.

Relationships were always a big problem in my life. You could call it another addiction. That's a nice little bow to put on it. But no matter how hard I tried, I just couldn't keep a relationship. I've reflected on this, I've been through years of therapy, and it's still something I struggle with. I knew I was a terrible husband to Wendy, and that knowledge was painful.

It was an awful time, but some great things came out of it too. In 2012, our sales hit one billion twenty-three million dollars, an unbelievable number. And I was thrilled that year when our daughter Goldie was born. She was an easy, happy baby with her own mind from the beginning, and she has retained that disposition to this day.

I soaked in my time with the kids. But after Goldie was born, it seemed like Wendy hated me. Nothing I did was right, and soon she started going to bed at nine o'clock at night just to get away from me. Of course it hadn't happened overnight, but it seemed that just as quickly as we'd fallen in love, it all fell apart.

12
BREAST

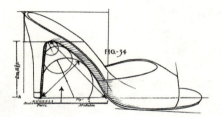

breast • the forward-facing part of the heel, under the arch of the sole.

My heart was pounding as I sat in the screening room waiting for *The Wolf of Wall Street* to begin. When I had first heard they were making Jordan's book into a movie, I was nervous. It's always fun to fantasize about your life being turned into a film, but this was a film focused on my biggest mistakes and from the point of view of my adversary. There was nothing fun about that.

At first, I just hoped the movie would be awful and no one would pay any attention to it. Then I found out Martin Scorsese was directing, and I knew that wouldn't be the case, so I simply prayed they would be kind to me in the telling.

I ended up being marginally involved in the film's production, but not enough to have any idea what the movie would end up being like. Maybe a year before, a producer had gotten in touch to see if they could shoot a scene in one of our stores. I was reluctant at first, but he assured me that I had nothing to worry about, and I decided it couldn't hurt to play along.

It was fascinating to watch the production team turn the clock back twenty years in our original SoHo store. They were only shooting a background scene with customers coming and going, but we still wanted every detail to be right. I helped arrange the shoe displays to look just like they had in 1993 and asked them to play The Counting Crows songs that we listened to all the time back then.

Being on the set was a cool experience, and sitting in the theater now, I was even more rapt by what I was watching on the screen: me as a young man played by Dustin Hoffman's son Jake, the actors portraying the Stratton brokers throwing shoes and heckling me exactly the way they had in real life, and Leonardo DiCaprio's spot-on depiction of Jordan. So much of the movie was eerily accurate. Watching it from the outside, it struck me how different that time in my life was from the way I lived now. These days, it was all about my kids, my sobriety, and work, of course. First things first.

At some point, without really noticing it, I started to relax. The movie was good. There was no question about that. It was funny and interesting, and I found myself laughing at certain scenes and watching others with curiosity, even though I knew what was going to happen. By the end, I breathed a huge sigh of relief. I have to say they were pretty easy on me. If anything, they downplayed my involvement in all of Jordan's shenanigans. And the bad deeds they did show me getting involved in were all things I'd already paid my price for and made my peace with. I left the screening feeling like a weight had been lifted. It was all going to be OK.

And sure enough, that movie ended up being good for me and for the company. Suddenly, people were interested in hearing about my life and my side of the story. Fans started asking less about my shoes and more about my past, and instead of being ashamed, I was happy to be out there as an example for people who'd made mistakes and were looking for a second chance.

The movie also raised our brand's awareness with young men and increased our name recognition. Nobody seemed to hold my mistakes against me; they thought it was cool that I'd gone through all that and come out on the other end better for it. There's a famous scene in the movie where Leo and Jonah Hill, playing Danny, are stoned on quaaludes and hilariously slur my name. Guys who had probably never heard of me before started coming up to me on the street and calling to me, "Steeeeeve Maaaaaadden!"

To this day, when I take Jack to a game at the Barclays Center, they introduce me on the Jumbotron by playing that scene. The crowd loves it, and I don't mind at all. Jordan's story is a part of mine, and that's just the way it is. Any resentment I may have had toward him for testifying against me is long gone. The government set up a scenario where the architect of the crime could tell on the people who carried out his plan. That's wrong. But Jordan did what he needed to do to save his own tail, and I forgive him.

As I've gotten older, I've stopped holding onto resentments the way I used to. Step four of the program is freedom from resentment, and it's a toughie. I used to love to fight and scrap and hold grudges, but when I can manage it, it does feel liberating to let go.

Plus, when you face real loss, the petty stuff gets right-sized, and it's easier to forgive. And *The Wolf of Wall Street* came out during a period of profound loss. After suffering from Alzheimer's for about ten years, my mother died in 2013. Wendy and I split up in 2014. And then John passed away in 2015 after a long battle with COPD.

I can't rank these, of course. They each carried their own pain. But John's death was particularly traumatic for me. Losing a sibling is a unique kind of loss. I still can't believe he's gone. My whole life, John was such a huge influence on me. It started with me looking up to him and ended with us being as close as brothers and then partners could be.

With both of my parents and John gone and Luke still in bad shape after his stroke, I felt alone, with no one left to connect me to my childhood and my family. As I suppose often happens at this stage of life, I turned to my kids for that sense of connection. They kept me sane and gave my life meaning. I always thought work was all that mattered. Before having kids, my life was singularly focused on my obsessive drive to "make it." But now I had to ask myself if that was really enough.

A lot of people were surprised when Wendy and I worked out a joint custody agreement after our split. They had assumed I would be the kind of dad who saw his kids on some weekends and holidays and left the bulk of the parenting to Wendy, but I wanted to be with the three of them as much as I possibly could. Losing John gave me a deeper appreciation of the time I had left. I knew that, when my time came, I wouldn't wish that I had worked more. I'd wish that I had spent more time with my kids.

I was nervous about moving out on my own, though. I hadn't lived alone since before going to prison, and I was never very good at it. It has always been impossible for me to keep track of things, and when I lived alone, my home always looked like a hovel.

To this day, I only manage to keep track of two things, and I'm embarrassed to tell you what they are. One is a pair of headphones that has to always be in the front right pocket of my jeans. If I move them even to another pocket, somehow I'll lose them. The other is a good luck charm that my friend and driver Alex gave me on the day I moved out of the townhouse I'd been living in with Wendy for ten years.

"My mom found this in Greece," he said, handing me an old-fashioned brass bottle opener with a Jewish star on it. "She wanted you to have it." That bottle opener is a little bulky and uncomfortable, but for me to start my day, it has to be in my front left pocket when I get dressed in the morning. It's sacrosanct.

But, of course, nothing keeps my life on track better than my kids themselves. There have been some bumps along the way, but Wendy and I have gotten into a good rhythm with our co-parenting. The kids are with me at least half of the time, and while it's hard as hell, I wouldn't have it any other way.

The small moments of parenting are torture and reward at once: getting up every morning much earlier than I'd like to make the kids toasted bagels with butter. I hate doing it, and I'm grumpy when I stumble my way to the toaster, still half asleep. But then the three of them are so happy munching on their bagels, and I feel proud that I accomplished something so simple. For that moment, all is well, and nothing else matters. Kids are freedom from the bondage of self.

At work, I experienced another loss at around this time. For nearly two decades, Rob Schmertz had been my creative partner and our brand director. I trusted him more than almost anyone, and he was simply the best at coming up with new styles and keeping up with trends. He was a huge part of Steve Madden's success, but his job was pressure-packed, and eventually it got to be too much.

In many ways, our relationship reminded me of the one I'd shared with John Basile, who helped take our production overseas way back when I was starting the business. Both John and Rob were tremendous collaborators. I respected both of them deeply. But there was always tension, and the feelings between us vacillated between love and hate practically on an hourly basis. Finally, in 2014, Rob decided to get out of the business.

This period of loss and a shifting of priorities included many gains for the company. We were rapidly expanding our fleet of stores in the United States and Canada and continuing to grow the business overseas. For the first time, this growth was spearheaded not by me, but by Ed and the rest of the team. That was radical itself.

Then, in 2014, all the deals we'd been making culminated but did not end with the acquisition of our biggest competitor. By that point, there was already a lot of history between Steve Madden and Dolce Vita. One of its founders, Van Lamprou, had briefly worked as a designer for us early in his career. And when I'd first gotten out of prison, they were making shoes for us while also maintaining their own brand. After a little while, they decided that they wanted to focus on building the Dolce Vita brand, so they stopped working with us.

As the Dolce Vita brand grew, they and Steve Madden became direct competitors. We were like warriors fighting each other every day for the same customers in stores like Nordstrom and Bloomingdale's that carried both brands. For a while, they were really giving us a run for our money, but then they hit a rough patch and put the company up for sale. We snapped it up right away.

This was a landmark deal. In the shoe business, it was practically the equivalent of Coke buying Pepsi because it gave us such a large share of the market. For the next few years, the top-selling young brands in department stores were Toms, Steve Madden, Dolce Vita, and Jessica Simpson. Now Toms has dropped off, and Jessica Simpson is still much smaller than the other brands. Since we owned the other two, we were able to dominate this space.

Through these years, we continued adding new celebrity partnerships and focused our marketing on social media, which helped us stay relevant to our young customers. This became an area of strength for the company, and in 2014 we partnered with Kendall and Kylie Jenner, the queens of social media, on a line of handbags and shoes for our Madden Girl brand, which was geared toward girls in their early teens.

"We grew up wearing Steve Madden," Kylie told me when we first met in Los Angeles. "I remember my first pair. They were black combat boots. I'm still obsessed with them today."

The Troopa. We'd released those in 2010, and they were still a huge hit around the globe.

"I was obsessed with them too," Kendall added. "And when I went to get them for myself, they were sold out."

Kendall and Kylie showed me pages they had ripped out of fashion magazines for inspiration. They had a lot of good ideas, and we tried to fit them all together to make a great package for the fans. When we debuted the line at Nordstrom, girls lined up for hours for a chance to meet Kendall and Kylie and have them sign their shoes.

Next up was a collaboration with Ja Rule, whom I'd met a few years earlier through the music producer Irv Gotti. I had been a fan of Ja's for a while. His song "New York" came out while I was in prison, and I had fond memories, as fond as memories from prison can be, of listening to it with the other guys.

Ja and I had more in common than people might have thought. We were both devoted dads, were both passionate about shoes, and had both spent time in prison. We started hanging out at Brooklyn Nets games, and eventually our conversations turned toward working together on a line of shoes.

Ja was a born entrepreneur. It was no accident that he'd been so successful in his career. And he backed up his strong personality with a great work ethic, two more things we had in common. Ja was highly involved in the design of the shoes. He wanted to incorporate details that spoke to both our struggles, like handcuff eyelets to represent being locked up in prison and skeleton keys to symbolize freedom and the keys to success. The shoes we created were comfortable, fun, and swaggy, and we were proud of them.

That same year, we teamed up with Iggy Azalea to create a line of shoes that included cool, brightly colored platforms and some chunky-heeled pumps. She was smart and great to work with, and everything was going well. Then we posted images of the shoes on social media, and Iggy posted on Twitter, calling the shots "disgusting," "God awful," and "gross." It was bizarre and totally undermined the success of the shoes she had worked so hard on. Unfortunately, we had to call it quits on the partnership after that first line.

Our next big acquisition in 2015 was Blondo, a hundred-year-old Canadian brand that made amazing waterproof leather boots. This deal happened without much input from me. Another milestone. Ed shepherded all our deals, but normally I played a big role in deciding which companies to acquire and then worked closely with Ed to make sure the deal went through. This time, Ed asked for my opinion but otherwise he just handled it while I focused on our celebrity collaborations and other ventures. I knew this was healthy, and I was proud of the team I'd put in place and coached that was now driving this growth. With them in charge, the company could continue without me after I was gone.

I wasn't planning on going anywhere, but there was no denying that I was getting older. I once heard someone say that we don't get older, but our bodies get older. That resonated with me. Inside, I still felt like the same obnoxious ten-year-old kid as always, but the casing had changed.

That year, I joined the team for a product meeting at our showroom. They started before I got there, and I could feel as soon as I walked through the door that I sucked all the energy out of the room. But I pushed on. They were talking about a pair of strappy sandals we had samples of in white and gold. I picked up a pair and turned to Rachelle. "Would you wear the gold?"

She nodded. "Yeah, we were just saying we should cancel the white and go with that one," she told me. "They're more wearable for the season."

"OK," I said. "What else you got?" She held up a pair of leopard mules. "Let me see the bottom." Those shoes reminded me of something, and I pulled out my phone. "I saw a great pair of leopard flats the other day," I told the team, scrolling as I tried to find a picture I had taken of a woman on the street. Well, of her feet.

"Here, look at this shoe," I said holding my phone out to Rachelle. "Can we do this in a skimmer?" Rachelle nodded. "This is a hot shoe," I continued, zooming in and out with my thumb and forefinger. "I love how it's a little pointy."

Michael Fishbein, an integral member of our team who runs our STEVEN line, leaned over the table to get a better look. "It's ugly," he said plainly.

"Who cares if it's ugly?" I asked him. "It's a hot shoe. Leopard is so hot now. Girls will be wearing this to the mall all spring."

Rachelle had left the room and was already back holding samples of all the shoes we had in leopard in one hand and the styles with the kind of shape I wanted in the other. "It's not the right time for it, but by the time it's ready the timing will be right," she said. I nodded, zooming in again on the picture on my phone. Then I looked up at the shoes Rachelle had in her hands.

"This one," I said, pointing to the leopard print that was the most similar to the shoes in the picture, and then pointed to another. "In this shape. Thank you."

"You got it," Rachelle said, and went off to make it happen.

"Man, Steve, I haven't seen you get that worked up about a shoe in a while," Michael said as soon as she was gone. He was right. It would be a good shoe. But at the same time, I knew I had only brought it up to make myself feel useful in that meeting, like I was still adding value.

Back when we were friends, Jordan taught me that the key to success was to delegate myself out of a job. This was something I never had any interest in doing. I enjoyed the daily worries and struggles too much. It was exciting and energizing and agonizing at the same time to be in the midst of creating something great. It felt like being on top of the world, the closest to true happiness I'd ever experienced.

Now I had won. The company was bigger and more successful than anyone could have predicted. I really *was* on the top of the world. And I missed the struggles it took to get there.

But holding on too tightly would only serve my ego and ultimately hold the company back. This was painful to accept. For nearly three decades, I'd been building and teaching my team, and now the pupils had outpaced the teacher. They were talented, driven professionals, and the truth is they no longer needed me. In some ways, I was a detriment to their success. It was time to face the fact that, in order for it to outlast me, I had to overcome my self-centeredness and let go of the company I'd given my life to create.

I confessed this to Eddie Lama the next morning. He had been retired for years when he told me that he was feeling bored, so I hired him
to do retail construction for Steve Madden. We were still close friends,
and every morning we did my old prison workout that Swole had taught
me together at the gym in our jeans and combat boots.

"They're better than me," I told him in between sets, wiping my head
with a towel. "And in a way this is how I designed it in my mind. Maybe
not as grandiose as all this, but I knew I could only do so much on my
own and found people to help me get the rest of the way there."

"That was very clever," Eddie told me. "But let me ask you something." He did a few extra pull-ups just to show off. "Isn't this how it's
supposed to be? You've built this great business, and you've got your
kids. Things are changing, and that's tough, but that's the way of the
world, my friend."

Eddie was right. I had money and success by any standard. So why
the hell was I still pushing? After all this time, I was still moved by the
need to grind, to find one more shred of self-worth in my next hit shoe.
But how many hit shoes would I need to create before I could believe that
I deserved this success? At the end of the day, that's got to be an inside
job. Until I felt it internally, I would never be enough.

The program teaches us, *being present helps me see the world in an authentic way.* I'd always been driven by the idea of what was next: the next
high, the next deal, and especially the next shoe. By focusing on the present, I could see that I had to find new ways to contribute to the company
and provide value instead of holding onto the past.

Ever since *The Wolf of Wall Street* had come out, young entrepreneurs
were reaching out to ask for my advice. When I did personal appearances
now, there were fewer young women asking me to sign their shoes and
more asking how I built this company from nothing into a
multi-billion-dollar global brand. At one appearance in Ann Arbor, a
college student raised her hand during the Q&A.

"I'm very proud of you," she told me when it was her turn at the mic. "You did a good job with your life."

I paused. She clearly meant no harm, but the implication of what she was saying was clear. "And now that it's over . . ." I said with a smile, winking to let her know that I wasn't really offended. The audience laughed. But as I moved on to the next question, I couldn't quite shake what she had said. She'd really gotten to me because she was so right. For me, the building and grinding and hustling really were in the past. My life wasn't over, but it wasn't about what I created in the moment anymore. It had to be about what I wanted to leave behind.

There were two things. One was a strong, dynamic company that was both profitable and a force for good. And the other was my life itself: my story, my mistakes, and the lessons I've learned along the way. The latter you're obviously holding in your hands. As for the former, I've found new ways to contribute within the company: by advising Ed on our deals, mentoring the team, and being a good influence, hopefully without making too much of a nuisance out of myself.

In 2019, I met a young guy named Ryan Babenzien who had started a digitally native sneaker company called Greats. Ryan reminded me so much of myself when I was his age: bright, with his eyes open and looking to disrupt the status quo. All the millennial men I encountered were talking about Greats, and acquiring the company gave us the opportunity to leverage their business model and elevate our men's business. The day after announcing this acquisition, we closed a deal to purchase BB Dakota, a trendy apparel company that is completely in tune with the Steve Madden girl.

I was excited about these new ventures, and there's even more on the horizon for Steve Madden. For years, I felt that our charge as a company was to design and produce fashionable shoes, get them to our customers quickly, and build a profitable company so we could hire people, pay them a good salary, and provide their families with healthcare. I saw this as the greater good.

Along the way, we changed the industry, making it faster and younger and more trend-focused. And an entire fast fashion movement sprung up around us. But the world keeps changing, and there's a bigger and more important movement happening now toward sustainability. I've got to be honest here: I resisted this for years. I didn't want to make a shift toward sustainability at the company's expense. If we have less of a carbon imprint but can no longer provide thousands of families with health insurance, is that worth it? For a long time, I didn't think so.

My goal has always been to give our customers what they wanted, and with so many people, including me, concerned about the environment, I realized that, for the first time, I was falling short by failing to keep up with a trend. My team would kill me for referring to sustainability as a trend. Call it a forever trend or a movement. But my point is that my "Steve Madden girls," the customers I know so well and have been obsessed with for my entire career, want a more sustainable shoe, so I have no choice but to give that to them. As the company that started fast fashion, we want to lead the way to making fast fashion more sustainable.

Maybe this sounds self-serving, like we're looking to capitalize on the sustainability movement. But the road to good deeds is often paved with selfish intentions. I'm the same self-centered guy I've always been. Now I choose the causes I give money to because of my own selfish desire for them to succeed. I help other people because I want them to have a second chance. And I'm going to make fast fashion sustainable because I want to stay on the forefront of trends.

In the program, we say that it doesn't matter why you come to meetings. Just keep coming back. And I do that for selfish reasons, too, because I love my kids, and I want to be there for them. I haven't won the war, and I never will. But every day, I'm still fighting.

With the pieces of my legacy in place, I'm free to spend time with my kids, contribute to the company in the ways that are exciting to me, and enjoy the fruits of my labor. That's what I try to do. *Being present helps me see the world in an authentic way.* In the present, when I manage to be there, I'm so happy and grateful for my life that it almost doesn't seem real. There are times when I'm eating a meal with the kids or playing with them in the pool, and I step outside of it for a moment and look at how beautiful they are, and I'm blown away.

But I haven't changed. And I don't want to. Like the pieces of a shoe, without each imperfect part of me, the full package would never be the same. My mistakes, my addiction, my weaknesses, my successes, and my family are all one. And true to form, when my thoughts slip to the future, I grow as fearful as always, like Chicken Little waiting for the sky to fall.

In that imagined future, I can see myself reminiscing about how great things used to be, back in the moment that's actually happening right now, when all the pieces of my life finally fit together, and for just one moment, I was whole.

ACKNOWLEDGMENTS